THE SPIRITUALS
AND THE BLUES

By the author:

A Black Theology of Liberation

My Soul Looks Back

For My People

Martin & Malcolm & America: A Dream or a Nightmare

Black Theology: A Documentary History (with Gayraud Wilmore)

Available from Orbis Books

James H. Cone

THE SPIRITUALS AND THE BLUES

An Interpretation

ORBIS BOOKS

Maryknoll, New York 10545

The Catholic Foreign Mission Society of America (Maryknoll) recruits and trains people for overseas missionary service. Through Orbis Books, Maryknoll aims to foster the international dialogue that is essential to mission. The books published, however, reflect the opinions of their authors and are not meant to represent the official position of the society.

Copyright © 1972, 1991 by James H. Cone

Original edition published by The Seabury Press, copyright © 1972

Published by Orbis Books, Maryknoll, NY 10545

Manufactured in the United States of America

Library of Congress Cataloging-in-Publication Data

Cone, James H.
    The spirituals and the blues : an interpretation / James H. Cone.
        p. cm.
    Includes bibliographical references.
    ISBN 0-88344-747-9 (pbk.)
    1. Afro-Americans—Music—History and criticism. 2. Spirituals
(Songs)—History and criticism. 3. Blues (Music)—History and
criticism. 4. Music—United States—History and criticism. 5. Afro-
Americans—Religion. I. Title.
ML3556.C66   1991
781.62'96073—dc20   91-19267
                                                                  CIP
                                                                  MN

To my sons
Michael and Charles

Contents

Preface

Without the encouragement and assistance of many persons, this book could not have been written. I am especially grateful to my black brothers and sisters who provided a critique, both positive and negative, of my earlier attempts to interpret the black religious experience and thus gave me the stimulus I needed for this present work.

A word of thanks is due to Lester Scherer of Eastern Michigan University. He read the manuscript and offered helpful editorial suggestions. Also I must express my gratitude to C. Eric Lincoln, my colleague at Union, and William Hordern, the president of Lutheran Theological Seminary. Both read the first draft of the manuscript and offered insightful criticism and encouragement.

I am grateful to Paul Lehmann, Lawrence Jones, Tom Driver, Roger Shinn, my colleagues at Union, and Cornish Rogers of the *Christian Century* for their reading of the manuscript.

Leon Watts, a doctoral student and tutor in Systematic Theology, also read the manuscript.

I must express my gratitude to Marilyn Cook who typed the manuscript twice, working overtime in order to meet the deadline for publication.

A special word of thanks is due to Rose, my wife. She worked very hard on the research for this book and also read the entire manuscript.

J. H. C.

Introduction

The power of song in the struggle for black survival—that is what the spirituals and blues are about. I grew up in a small black community in Bearden, Arkansas, where black music was essential for identity and survival. On Saturday nights the juke box was loud, and one could hear the sound and feel the rhythm of the blues even from a distance. The men and women gathered around the juke box had worked long hours during the week in saw mills and factories; by Saturday night they were tired and weary. They needed to express their moods and feelings, their joys and sorrows. They needed to refresh their spirits in the sound and rhythm of black humanity. And they did, sometimes peaceably and sometimes violently, often doing to each other what they wished they could do to white people. But chiefly they enjoyed themselves. Little Milton was always a favorite, especially his lines:

> If I don't love you baby,
> Grits ain't grocery,
> Eggs ain't poultry
> And Mona Lisa was a man.

Yes, the Spirit was indeed high, when these black people were swinging to the sound and rhythm of the blues.

But not every black in Bearden responded spontaneously to Little Milton and his interpretation of the blues. These latter preferred the other musical expression of black people, called "church music" or the spirituals, and Sunday was their time to unleash the pent-up emotions of their being. At Macedonia A.M.E. Church, the Spirit of God was no abstract concept, no vague perception of philosophical speculation. The Spirit was

the "power of God unto salvation," that "wheel in the middle
of the wheel." The Spirit was God breaking into the lives of the
people, "buildin' them up where they were torn down and prop-
pin' them up on every leanin' side." The Spirit was God's presence with the people and God's will to provide them the courage
and the strength to make it through. And the people were thank-
ful for God's presence and renewed weekly their covenant to
"hold out to the end." I can hear it now—my mother is singing
her favorite song:

> This little light of mine,
> I'm goin' to let it shine;
> This little light of mine,
> I'm goin' to let it shine,
> Let it shine, let it shine.
>
> Everywhere I go,
> I'm goin' to let it shine;
> Everywhere I go,
> I'm goin' to let it shine,
> Let it shine, let it shine.
>
> God give it to me,
> I'm goin' to let it shine;
> My God give it to me,
> I'm goin' to let it shine,
> Let it shine, let it shine.

At Macedonia A.M.E. Church the melody, rhythm, and style
were black; the mood was black; and the people were black.
Everything they did was a valiant attempt to define and structure
the meaning of blackness—so that their children and their children's children would be a little "freer" than they were. They
had a "hard row to hoe" and a "rocky road to travel," and they
had made it and intended to make it "through the storm."

It is not, however, the story of black music in Bearden that
will occupy central place in what follows, but the larger story of
black music as expressed in the spirituals and the blues—these
songs, their meaning and depth, is what I want to talk about.

I want to examine the spirituals and the blues as cultural expressions of black people, having prime significance for their community. How did the involuntary servitude of Africans and their descendants in America reflect itself in the music? What were the techniques employed for cultural survival?

I also want to reflect on the theological and sociological implications of these songs. What did it mean "to steal away to Jesus" when one had been *stolen* from Africa and enslaved in white America? What did it mean to "work on a building that is a true foundation" or to "hold up the blood-stained banner for the Lord" when one had no building to call his or her own, and one's own blood was stained with slavery? What did it mean to be a "child of God" and a black slave in a white society? All these questions touch the very substance and "gut" of black religion as reflected in the spirituals.

And then there were the blues singers—Blind Lemon Jefferson, Bessie Smith, and B. B. King. What are we to make of their faith?

> Woke up dis mornin' feelin' sad and blue,
> Woke up dis mornin' feelin' sad and blue,
> Didn't have nobody to tell my trouble to.

What is the blues' relationship to the spirituals, and how do they relate to segregation, lynchings, and the political disfranchisement of black people? What do the blues tell us about the black strivings for being?

I must confess that I am not an unbiased interpreter of the spirituals and the blues. It simply was not possible to grow up with the Arkansas blues and the spirituals of Macedonia A.M.E. Church and remain unaffected by the significance of blackness in the context of white society. I am therefore convinced that it is not possible to render an authentic interpretation of black music without having shared and participated in the experience that created it. Black music must be *lived* before it can be understood.

Of course, I do not deny that there are "objective" data which are available to any student of black music and history, and it is possible to draw certain conclusions on the basis of that data.

But I contend that there is a deeper level of experience which transcends the tools of "objective" historical research. And that experience is available only to those who share the *spirit* and participate in the *faith* of the people who created these songs. I am referring to the power and energy released in black devotion to the God of emotion.

Consider the spiritual

> Every time I feel the spirit
> Moving in my heart I will pray.
> Every time I feel the spirit
> Moving in my heart I will pray.
>
> Upon the mountain my Lord spoke
> Out of His mouth came fire and smoke.
> In the valley on my knees,
> Asked my Lord, Have mercy, please.
>
> Every time I feel the spirit
> Moving in my heart I will pray . . .

To interpret the religious significance of that spiritual for the black community, "academic" tools are not enough. The interpreter must *feel* the Spirit; that is, one must feel one's way into the power of black music, responding both to its rhythm and the faith in experience it affirms. This song invites the believer to move close to the very sources of black existence, and to experience the black community's power to endure and the will to survive. The mountains may be high and the valleys low, but "my Lord spoke" and "out of his mouth came fire and smoke." All the believer has to do is to respond to the divine apocalyptic disclosure of God's revelation and cry, "Have mercy, please." This cry is not a cry of passivity, but a faithful, free response to the movement of God's Spirit. It is the black community accepting themselves as the people of the Spirit and knowing through that presence that no chains can hold the Spirit of black humanity in bondage. LeRoi Jones is right: "The God spoken about in the black songs is not the same one in the white songs. Though the words might look the same. (They are not even pronounced alike.) But it is a different quality of energy they summon."[1]

Black music is unity music. It unites the joy and the sorrow, the love and the hate, the hope and the despair of black people; and it moves the people toward the direction of total liberation. It shapes and defines black existence and creates cultural structures for black expression. Black music is unifying because it confronts the individual with the truth of black existence and affirms that black being is possible only in a communal context.

Black music is functional. Its purposes and aims are directly related to the consciousness of the black community. To be functional is to be useful in community definition, style, and movement. That is why B. B. King says:

> *Blues* is B. B. King. Yes, and I've been a crusader for it for 21 years. Without this, I don't think I could *live* very long—not that I think I'm goin' to live a long time anyway, but I don't think I could live even *that* long if I had to stop playin' or if I couldn't be with the people I love so, the people that have *helped* me so much. . . . I couldn't *live*! I try to give them a message. I try *hard*.[2]

B. B. King is not alone in acknowledging the inseparable bond that exists between black life and black art so that the art is a natural function of the life. Charlie Parker, the jazz musician, makes the same point: "Music is your own experience, your thoughts, your wisdom. If you don't live it, it won't come out of your horn."[3]

Black music is a living reality. And to understand it, it is necessary to grasp the contradictions inherent in black experience. Who could possibly understand these paradoxical affirmations but the people who live them?

> I love the blues, they hurt so nice.

> I can't stand you, Baby, but I need you,
> You're bad, but you're oh so good.

Black music is also social and political. It is social because it is *black* and thus articulates the separateness of the black com-

munity. It is an artistic rebellion against the humiliating dead-
ness of western culture. Black music is political because in its
rejection of white cultural values, it affirms the political "oth-
erness" of black people. Through song, a new political consciousness is continuously created, one antithetical to the values
of white society.

Black music is also theological. That is, it tells us about the
divine Spirit that moves the people toward unity and self-deter-
mination. It is not possible to be black and encounter the Spirit
of black emotion and not be moved. My purpose is to uncover
the theological presuppositions of black music as reflected in
the spirituals and the blues, asking: What do they tell us about
black people's deepest aspiration and devotion? I will ask questions about God, Jesus Christ, life after death, and suffering;
and I will seek to investigate these questions in the light of black
people's historical strivings for freedom.

A word about the obvious limitations of this book. I have
limited discussion to the spirituals that were influenced by the
black experience of slavery and to the early period of develop-
ment of the blues. Though I have not always remained within
this strict limitation, references to recent developments in black
music are rare. Specifically, I first review some important eval-
uative interpretations of the slave songs (Chapter 1) before
undertaking a theological interpretation (Chapters 3, 4, and 5)
that is based on the sociohistorical experience of black people
in the late eighteenth and nineteenth centuries (Chapter 2). The
blues (Chapter 6) enter the picture as a late parallel develop-
ment with a seemingly different perspective. My purpose is to
examine the statement of black experience in the blues as compared with that in the spirituals, investigating their similarities
and dissimilarities from both theological and historical view-
points.

Existentially, the subject matter and focus of this book have
been defined by the black musical forms which have influenced
my life. I have written about the spirituals and the blues because
I have lived the experience which created them. In Bearden, the
spirituals and the blues were a way of life, an artistic affirmation
of the meaningfulness of black existence. No black person could
escape the reality they expressed. B. B. King, Johnny Lee

Hooker, and Mahalia Jackson created essential structures that defined my blackness. I affirmed the reality of the spirituals and blues as authentic expressions of my humanity, responding to them in the rhythms of dance. I, therefore, write about the spirituals and the blues, because *I am the blues* and my *life is a spiritual.* Without them, I cannot be.

1

Interpretations of the Black Spirituals

Serious comment upon the black spirituals is scarcely a hundred years old. During that time, however, the slave songs have been assessed from a surprising variety of directions. It is important to note briefly this history of scholarly interpretation, in order to define the scope of the present study.

The Debate about Black Music

The earliest comments and debates centered—perhaps too predictably—around the music of the spirituals. The earliest major collector of black music, William Francis Allen, was surprised that "no systematic effort [had] been made to collect and preserve" the slave songs, since "the musical capacity of the negro race [had] been recognized for so many years."[1] Like many white Northerners of that period and thereafter, he assumed that the creative musical expression of the spirituals was self-evident, even though he described the black creators as "half-barbarous people." It never occurred to him that art and thought cannot be separated; and thus there is something contradictory about the idea of "discovering the rich vein of music that existed in these half-barbarous people."[2] Although he recognized correctly the musical creativity of the slave songs, his own cultural experience precluded his encounter with the deeper level of human experience reflected in the spirituals.

9

Although many whites, like Allen, granted "musical genius" as the sole distinction of an otherwise degraded race, some were unwilling to allow even that. Most notable among these detractors of black music was the German musicologist Richard Wallaschek. In his book, *Primitive Music* (1893) he said that black songs were "mere imitations of European compositions which negroes have picked up and served up again with slight variations."[3] And referring specifically to the Allen, Ware, and Garrison collection, he said that he did not "think these and the rest of the songs deserve the praise given by the editors, for they are unmistakably 'arranged'— not to say ignorantly borrowed— from the national songs of all nations, from military signals, well-known marches, German student songs, etc."[4] For one reason or another few scholars sided with Wallaschek, whose racial motivation was quite evident in his writings. His book, nevertheless, created much debate about the originality of slave music.

One of the first negative responses to Wallaschek's view came from Henry Krehbiel, a white musical expert. In a perceptive analysis, he attempted to prove that the slave songs were "the only considerable body of song which has come into existence"[5] in America, and that they were the authentic music of black people. John W. Work, James Weldon Johnson, and Alain Locke joined Krehbiel in attacking Wallaschek.

Work, a professor of music at Fisk University, concentrated on the originality of the slave music, attempting to uncover the African background of the spirituals. The heat of his attack on Wallaschek's white-to-black thesis reveals Work's personal attachment to the slave songs.

"Imitations!" It would be folly to attempt to deny the fact that the American Negro's music shows some resemblance to the music of other peoples. . . . But to assert that he [Wallaschek] has found any greater resemblance between the Negro's music and European music than would naturally result from the oneness of human nature, lays the writer open to the suspicion that he is uninformed, misinformed, superficial, unscientific, or all of these.

"Variations!" . . . It may be that Dr. Wallaschek has

heard the Negro sing the "long meters" of Dr. Watt and other hymn writers. If so, he certainly heard such variations as never man heard before! For the Negro is able to take one of these hymns and sing it in such voice that it will seem more than a "European composition, picked up and served up again with slight variations," for he can run up and down the scale, make side trips and go off on furloughs, all in time and in such perfectly dazzling ways as to bewilder the uninitiated.[6]

Johnson, like Work, rejected the white-to-black thesis asserting that the spirituals are "America's only folk music and . . . the finest distinctive artistic contribution she has to offer."[7] He denied the possibility of influence from Scotland or Russia, but admitted that slaves may have been influenced by their masters. He observed, however, that

> if ignorant Negroes evolved such music as *Deep River, Steal Away to Jesus, Somebody's Knockin' at Yo' Do', I Couldn't Hear Nobody Pray* and *Father Abraham* by listening to their masters sing gospel hymns, it does not detract from the achievement but magnifies it.[8]

Alain Locke also asserted the originality and distinctive richness of the black music. Its beauty, he declared, is not limited by race consciousness but affirms a universal ideal for the whole American nation.[9]

The discussion of the cultural antecedents of the slave songs was enriched from the twenties onward by specialized studies that combined the skills of musicology and anthropology. The debate came to center upon the issue of "Africanisms" or "African survivals" among slaves in the United States. On the one hand the monographs of Newman White,[10] Guy Johnson,[11] and George Pullen Jackson[12] which compared the white and black spirituals of the nineteenth century, showed the difficulties of making a case for the exclusive African origin of the spirituals. On the other hand the pioneering work of Melville Herskovits[13] on Africanisms and the later articles of Sterling Brown on the slave songs, reveal the serious limitations of the white-to-black thesis. Brown takes both extremes into account and concludes that:

A give-and-take seems logical to expect. Correspondences between white and Negro melodies have been established. The complete Africanism of the spirituals was never tenable. The spirituals are obviously not in an African musical idiom, not even so much as the music of Haiti, Cuba, and Brazil. But all of this does not establish the Negro spiritual ... as imitative of white music, or as unoriginal, or as devoid of traces of the African idiom. ... The obstinate fact of a great difference between Negro folk-songs and the white camp-meeting hymns exists. Even the strongest adherents of the view that the origin of the Negro spirituals is in white music, agree that now the spiritual is definitely the Negro's own and, regardless of birthplace, is stamped with originality[14]

Certainly there is limited usefulness in a debate over the degree of originality in the slave songs. It was, of course, outrageous that the artistic creativity of black musicians should be denied or belittled by anyone, and such contemptuous assessments of black music had (and have) to be answered whenever they appeared. Nonetheless, from the viewpoint of a black ethos there was a built-in limitation upon a debate centering upon artistry in a society that generally belittles art anyway. Whites could grant that blacks were great musicians without ceasing to deny them membership in American society.

The Souls of Black Folk

As an interpreter of the spirituals, W. E. B. DuBois stands in a class alone. Not only was his essay, "Of the Sorrow Songs" (1903), the first significant interpretation of the slave spirituals, but it is so rich in feeling and observation that it defies classification. That little piece, which was the closing chapter of *The Souls of Black Folk*, towered over the intermittent debate about the originality of black music. DuBois' essay set the stage for other serious study and comment on the spirituals while always remaining the irreplaceable gem of interpretation.

DuBois was happy to place his weight on the side of the distinctive character of the slave songs, characterizing them as the "sole American music." But he went far beyond that and related the songs to the cultural history of black people striving for humanity in a society of oppression and racial hatred. They were the "most beautiful expression of human experience born this side of the seas."[15] He called them sorrow songs, because they were "the music of an unhappy people, of the children of disappointment; they tell of death and suffering and unvoiced longing toward a truer world, of misty wanderings and hidden ways."[16]

However, DuBois perceived something else in the beauty of the spirituals—an affirmation of life. "Through all of the sorrow of the Sorrow Songs there breathes a hope—a faith in the ultimate justice of things." Despite the presence of slavery and the oppression of people because of skin color, there is the faith that "sometime, somewhere, men will judge men by their souls and not by their skins." DuBois wondered how slaves could affirm such a time and place, when there was no external, historical evidence to support their confidence. "Is such a hope justified? Do the Sorrow Songs sing true?"[17]

DuBois was fascinated by the tension in the spirituals between hope and despair, joy and sorrow, death and life, and by the ability of black slaves to embrace such polarities in their music. In his own struggle "to attain self-conscious manhood, to merge his double self into a better and truer self,"[18] DuBois came to know through the spirituals that the black slaves had travelled the road before him. He was impressed by their struggle and their faith that "trouble don't last always."

Social and Historical Perspectives

In an article entitled "The Social Implications of the Negro Spiritual," John Lovell introduced another approach to the study of the black spiritual. According to Lovell, the "spiritual is essentially social,"[19] and his concern was to uncover "the vast wealth of the spiritual in terms of the social mind of a very powerful social unit."[20] He accordingly examined the slave songs in the light of the social consciousness of the black slave. The social mind of the slaves was a reflection of their African background, their life on southern plantations, and their encounter with slave masters, overseers, auctioneers, and buyers. The songs were a reflection of this existence, and of the measures used to deal with the dehumanization inherent in it.

Lovell especially emphasized the physical and mental resistance to slavery. The slave songs reveal the social consciousness of blacks who refused to accept white limitations placed on their lives. Lovell rejected the idea that the slave songs were simply religious and otherworldly projections toward a transcendent reality unrelated to the sociality of slave existence. Rather, the black spirituals were "the slave's description and criticism of his environment" and "the key to his revolutionary sentiments and to his desire to fly to free territory."[21]

Lovell repudiated the view that interpreted the spiritual merely from the religious perspective, as if the religion of the slave was an isolated phenomenon, unrelated to the desire for social and political freedom. Black slaves were "not the kind of people to think unconcretely; and the idea that they put all their eggs into the basket of a heaven after death, as the result of abstract thinking, is absurd to any reader of firsthand materials in the social history of the slave."[22] He brought Douglass and Turner to the stand as evidence that religion took "weird turns" when placed in the hands of black slaves in touch with a worth that transcended abstract, theological thought. To be sure, "Nat Turner was a preacher and he knew his Bible well"; but he did not let his religion distort his perceptions of the sociality of slave existence, "for it led him to bloody massacres, coldly planned." Frederick Douglass also refused to accept the religious ideas of his master, since they did not "improve his attitude toward his slaves."[23]

Lovell's concern was not to question the integrity of slave religion but to relate it to the social life of the black slave struggle for freedom in this life. He perceived three central themes in the black spiritual: (1) a desire for freedom; (2) a "desire for justice in the judgment upon his betrayers"; and (3) "a tactic battle, the strategy by which he expected to gain an eminent future."[24]

Drawing upon these themes, Lovell interpreted references to Satan, Jesus, and heaven as concrete possibilities for earthly freedom. Satan was "the people who beat and cheat the slave," and King Jesus was "whoever helps the oppressed and disfranchised or gives him a right to his life." "Hell [was] often being sold South," and "Jordan [was] the push for freedom."[25] In the spirituals "I Got Shoes," "When I Get to Heaven," "Swing Low," and "My Lord Delivered Daniel," the black slave was "tearing down a wreck and building a new, solid world, and all along we thought he was romanticizing."[26]

Miles Mark Fisher offers another helpful analysis in his study of the spirituals, which provides a historical context which is important for any theological interpretation of the slave songs. According to Fisher, "the so-called 'slave songs' of the United States are best understood when they are considered as expressions of individual Negroes which can be dated and assigned to a geographical locale."[27] Like Lovell, he places the otherworldly emphasis in its proper context. The spirituals are the story of black people's historical strivings for earthly freedom, rather than the otherworldly projections of hopeless Africans who forgot about their homeland. The songs tell a historical story of "how Negroes attempted to spread brotherhood by the sword, took flight to 'better' territory when possible, became pacific in the United States, and laid hold upon another world as a last resort."[28]

The contention that the spirituals are "historical documents" is based on the assumption that they are African and not European, since "the chief concern of African music was to recite the history of the people."[29] Therefore, when Africans were brought to America, they carried with them the art of storytelling through music. The black spirituals then are a reflection mainly of "African background patterns" rather than white American Christianity.

Much of Fisher's interpretation is devoted to uncovering the origin and first intention of the songs. For example, he contends that the spirituals "Sinner, Please Don't Let This Harvest Pass" and "Let Us Praise God Together On Our Knees" probably referred to a slave resistance meeting that was more African than Christian.[30] He dates both between 1740 and 1815. The song "Deep River, My Home Is Over Jordan" referred to the possibility of crossing over to Africa.[31] And the spiritual "Steal Away" served as a means to convene secret meetings during the early part of the nineteenth century, its probable composer being Nat Turner.[32]

While one may hold some reservations concerning the historical evidence for pinpointing the details of composition, there is no doubt of the significance of Fisher's study. He is persuasive in his contention that many spirituals referred originally to concrete historical events and that their language could, therefore, be transferred to later events, expressing similar responses to similar situations. Fisher reminds us that there is another side to apparently otherworldly poetry.

Religion in the Spirituals

Both Lovell and Fisher dealt with religion in their studies, but it remained rather at the edges of their respective central concerns. Howard Thurman was one of the first scholars to use religion as the starting point in his interpretation of the black spirituals. "The clue to the meaning of the spirituals is to be found in religious experience and spiritual discernment." In the spirituals, he perceives "the elemental and formless struggle to a vast consciousness in the mind and spirit of the individual."[33]

According to Thurman, the black spiritual is an expression of the slaves' determination to *be* in a society that seeks to destroy their personhood. It is an affirmation of the dignity of the black slaves, the essential humanity of their spirits. Where human life is regarded as property and death has no dignity, "the human spirit is stripped to the literal substance of itself."[34] Deprived of power, the slaves found ways to hold together their personhood. To be sure, the insights reflected in the slaves' struggle for being may not have been original, but "in the presence of the naked demand upon the primary sources of meanings, even without highly specialized tools or skills, the universe responded . . . with overwhelming power."[35]

The essence of ante-bellum black religion was the emphasis on the *somebodiness* of black slaves. The content of the black preacher's message stressed the essential worth of their person.

"You are created in God's image. You are not slaves, you are not 'niggers'; you are God's children."[36] Because religion defined the *somebodiness* of their being, black slaves could retain a sense of the dignity of their person even though they were treated as things. Death was a fact of existence which could become a reality at the slightest whim of slave masters; but since God is the sovereign ruler, death cannot be the master of life. Through the songs, black slaves affirmed the universal dimensions of the human spirit and its transcendence over the vicissitudes of life.

Despite the profundity of Thurman's essay on the essentially religious character of the spirituals, he did not attempt the full scope of theological analysis. Ironically it was the sociologist Benjamin Mays who became the first (and virtually the only) scholar to analyze the slave songs under theological categories.[37] Summarizing the concept of God in the songs, Mays says that God is omnipotent, omnipresent, and omniscient,[38] and he is sovereign in heaven and on earth. God is just—"just to the point of cruelty"—destroying the wicked in hell and vindicating the righteous by offering a reward in heaven. The righteous receive "golden crowns, slippers, robes and eternal life" for holding out to the end. Those who endure trouble and pain in this world will receive rest and peace in the next world—if they do not lose faith. According to Mays, the distinctive characteristic of the spirituals is the "compensatory idea, that God will bring His own out victoriously in the end."[39]

God is a God who answers prayers; and "it makes no difference . . . what the situation is, 'A little talk wid Jesus makes it right.' "[40] According to Mays, the spirituals affirm a complete trust in God to make right in the next world what was done wrong in this world. God is the Judge who writes down the right and wrong acts of human beings according to the standard recorded in the Bible. And eventually all men and women will have to stand before God and give an account of their ethical behavior on earth. Thus, in Mays' view, the spirituals provided an emotional security for oppressed slaves during turbulent times. Since they had no economic or political security in this world, they put their trust in Jesus whom they believed would make everything all right.

Heaven, hell, and judgment are central ideas in the black

spirituals, according to Mays. Heaven is the home of the faithful which has been prepared outside of history for God's righteous servants. It is the place of the "great camp meeting in the Promised Land." Judgment is the day of reckoning, a time for the accounting of one's deeds on earth. Whoever remains obedient and does not give in to the evil ways of Satan will be received by God in his glory. The wicked will be condemned to hell. These ideas, like the idea of God, are compensatory in their nature and function. "They adhere to the compensatory pattern because they are ideas that enable Negroes to endure hardships, suffer pain, and withstand maladjustment, but they do not necessarily motivate them to strive to eliminate the source of the ills they suffer." They are otherworldly because "they lead one to repudiate this world, consider it a temporary abode, and look to Heaven for a complete realization of the needs and desires that are denied expression here."[41]

Contrary to Lovell and Fisher, Mays sees little emphasis on this world in the songs. To be sure, Mays would not deny that there are some social and historical implications in the spirituals, but they are few. Such songs as "Go Down, Moses," "Oh, Freedom," and "No More, No More, No More Auction Block For Me" are signs of rebellion "against earthly conditions without seeking relief in Heaven."[42] But such spirituals do not represent the majority. Generally speaking, the spirituals "kept the slaves submissive, humble, and obedient."[43] They emphasized that blacks should not fight the oppressors, but should take their burdens to the Lord and leave them there. God will heal the pain and bind the broken heart. No need to worry about white folk, their money, laws, or armies, for God is our Leader, and God will make a way out of no way. God will uplift the weak and put down the strong—all in God's own good time and in God's own way. All the slaves had to do was to wait on God and not get weary about their suffering. In the end, God will make everything all right.

Although Mays' interpretation is theological, his analysis suffers from too much emphasis on the otherworldly and compensatory character of the songs, without considering the possibility of other levels of thought embedded in them. Indeed "compensatory" is not a theological term at all, and one may wonder if it is a sociologist's tool for tucking all theology into an insignificant corner. In any case there is much more to say about the theology of these songs.

My contention is that there is a complex world of *thought* underlying the slave songs that has so far escaped analysis. Further theological interpretation is needed to uncover this thought and the fundamental world view that it implies. It will no longer suffice to bundle up the spirituals with a label like "compensatory," "childlike," or even "beautiful," while ignoring the very essence of what they were attempting to communicate.

2

The Black Spirituals and Black Experience

*I can tell you that the life of an average slave
was not rosy. —An ex-slave.*

No theological interpretation of the black spirituals can be valid that ignores the cultural environment that created them. The black experience in America is a history of servitude and resistance, of survival in the land of death. It is the story of black life in chains and of what that meant for the souls and bodies of black people. This is the experience that created the spirituals, and it must be recognized if we are to render a valid theological interpretation of these black songs.

The exact origins of African slavery on this continent are obscure. The first Africans were sold in Jamestown in 1619, but probably not as perpetual slaves. It is quite clear, however, that by 1700 the status of most Africans in North America was settled: they were slaves for life, and their children inherited that condition. Africans were presumed by Europeans to be especially in need of the strict control provided by the slave regime. In American law and custom the dark skin carried the presumption of degradation and slavery. America became the land of freedom for white people only; for blacks it was the land of bondage.

Slavery meant being snatched from your homeland and sailing to an unknown land in a stinking ship. Slavery meant being regarded as property, like horses, cows, and household goods. For blacks the auction block was one potent symbol of their subhuman status. The block stood for "brokenness," because on sale days no family ties were recognized. "My brothers and sisters were bid off first, and one by one," recalled Josiah Henson, "while my mother, paralyzed by grief, held me by the hand." When Moses Grandy's wife was sold, he was permitted only to stand at a distance and speak with her before she was taken away. "My heart was so full," he remembered, "that I could say very little." Slavery meant working fifteen to twenty hours a day and being beaten for showing fatigue. It meant being driven into the field three weeks after delivering a baby. It meant having the cost of replacing you calculated against the value of your labor during a peak season, so that your owner could decide whether to work you to death. It meant being whipped for crying over a fellow slave who had been killed while trying to escape.

It has been observed that American law was not consistent in viewing slaves as property. In some measure their personhood was acknowledged, as in laws requiring owners to feed them, clothe them, take care of them in sickness and old age, and not capriciously kill or maim them. Under the law, then, slaves were property *and* persons. But the two definitions together were absurd. The concept of property negated the idea of personhood. To be a person is to be in control of one's destiny, to set certain concrete limitations on the movement of self and of other selves in relation to self. It is to be free—to work or not to work, to laugh and cry, to make love, to eat and sleep at the close of the day. All this implies a measure of power to make others recognize one's humanity. But that power was precisely what the slave regime could not grant, because it compromised the economic control and personal security of the owner class. To be property means, after all, to have one's existence determined solely by one's owner. Slaves were seldom permitted to testify in court against white abuse, so that apparently humane statutes were dead letters. Personhood was acknowledged mainly by holding slaves accountable for their "crimes." To acknowledge the personhood of slaves in more positive ways would have undermined not only the wealth of the masters but also their inflated self-esteem, whereby they could justify the utter exploitation of slaves by "civilized" whites as a blessing to the blacks.

Just as it is absurd to speak of consistent protection of the personhood of slaves, so it is meaningless to talk about "good" masters. Historically, there were different degrees of harshness and different methods of exercising mastery. But the community of slavery's victims can never say that there were good masters any more than there are good murderers or good racists. Black wisdom destroys the illusion of good masters.

> I's hear tell of them good slave days, but I ain't never seen no good times then.[1]

> Lord, Lord, honey! Them was awful days.[2]

> Slavery time was tough, boss. You don't know how tough it was. I can't 'splain to you just how bad all the niggers want to get their freedom.[3]

> Tisn't he who has stood and looked on, that can tell you what slavery is, — 'tis he who has endured.[4]

Of course, some blacks said otherwise. But that only means that the "good" masters were in fact the worst, if we consider the dehumanizing effect of mental servitude.[5] At least those who were blatant in their physical abuse could not so easily dominate the minds of black people. When white savagery was plain and open, it was easier for blacks to define themselves as autonomous human beings rather than as appendages of white owners. The "house niggers" (not all domestic servants were in this category) were those who internalized white values and betrayed their fellow blacks. The masters' efforts to induce such mental servitude was perhaps the worst of their crimes, and the "kind" ones did it best.

We should be reminded here of the role played by white Christianity in producing mental servitude among blacks. Through most of the eighteenth century planters were generally suspicious of white people who wanted to "christianize" the slaves. Gradually, however, many owners came to feel that "the deeper the piety of the slave, the more valuable he is in every respect."[6] An Alabama judge said that Christianity "not only benefits the slave in his moral relations, but enhances his value as an honest, faithful servant and laborer."[7] These people perceived that "sound religious instruction" could assist mightily in producing docile slaves. Slave catechisms were written to insure that the message of black inferiority and divinely ordained white domination would be instilled in the slaves.

Q. What did God make you for?
A. To make a crop.
Q. What is the meaning of "Thou shalt not commit adultery"?
A. To serve our heavenly Father, and our earthly master, obey our overseer, and not steal anything.[8]

It does not take a seminary education to know that white missionaries and preachers were distorting the gospel in order to defend the enslavement of blacks. And what is more revealing is that few white theologians and clergy, either Protestant or Catholic, spoke out against the heresy of white Christianity. By and large, the intellectuals either ignored the problem of human servitude or sided with the pro-slavery attitude.[9] Black slaves were condemned to live in a society where not only the government but "God" condoned their slavery. The spirituals were created out of that environment.

However, if black history were no more than the story of what whites did to blacks, there would have been no spirituals. Black history is also the record of black people's resistance, an account of their perceptions of their existence in an oppressive society. What whites did to blacks is secondary. The primary reality is what blacks did to whites in order to delimit the white assault on their humanity.

When white people enslaved Africans, their intention was to dehistoricize black existence, to foreclose the possibility of a future defined by the African heritage. White people demeaned black people's sacred tales, ridiculing their myths and defiling the sacred rites. Their intention was to define humanity according to European definitions so that their brutality against Africans could be characterized as civilizing the savages. But white Europeans did not succeed; and black history is the record of their failure. Black people did not stand passively by while white oppressors demoralized their being. Many rebelled physically and mentally. Black history in America is the history of that rebellion.

Black rebellion in America did not begin with the Civil Rights movement and Martin Luther King, nor with Black Power and Stokely Carmichael or the Black Panther Party. Black resistance has roots stretching back to the slave ships, the auction blocks, and the plantation regime. It began when the first black person decided that death would be preferable to slavery. If white people could just realize this, then they might be able to understand Malcolm X and other black revolutionaries. White people should know about Gabriel Prosser, Denmark Vesey, and Nat Turner and their efforts to break the chains of slavery.[10] They should know about Harriet Tubman and her liberation of more than 300 black slaves.[11] They should know about David Walker and Henry Garnet and their urgent call for rebellion and resistance among the slaves.[12] Until recently there was a tendency among historians to ignore the fact of slave resistance, preferring to believe that blacks completely internalized the white masters' values. We know now that whatever is said about mental servitude, docility is not the whole story. For if slaves were as harmless as whites contended, why was there almost universal fear about slave insurrections? The fact is that much of the fear was well grounded. Black slaves were not passive, and black history is the record of their resistance against the condition of human bondage.

However, the majority of the slaves did not pursue the path of physical violence, because they knew that their chances of gaining freedom against patrols, militia, or the regular army were minimal. They chose other forms of resistance. The most common was to take the risk of fleeing to "free" territory in the North or Canada. There were thousands of runaways, and many lived to tell of their adventures through flight.[13] Who were these runaways? They represented every segment of slave life: the young and the old, the house and the field slaves, the blacks and the mulattoes, the "kindly" treated, and those who bore the scars of the masters' cruelty. Some masters who had delusions about their own goodness and the contentedness of their slaves could not understand why slaves ran away. "Poor ignorant devils, for what do they run away? They are well clothed, work easy, and have all kinds of plantation produce."[14] Such reactions are typical of those who do not *know* the reality of serfdom.

"Why do they run away?" The answer is simple. Blacks ran away because they disliked other people holding them in bondage. Some wanted to re-establish their families broken on the auction block. Others could not stand any longer the physical and mental brutality of the masters' authority. Still others heard of Harriet Tubman and the Underground Railroad and decided to accept the risk and adventure of struggling for freedom. Then again, many blacks just could not accept the condition of servitude as a philosophical and theological possibility for human beings; and they decided to reshape their history according to black possibilities. The reasons for running away varied from slave to slave, and it is impossible to catalogue all of their motives. What we do know is that the underlying assumption which made flight a possibility stemmed from an affirmation of black identity as defined by slaves and not by those who attempted to rule over them. As one black slave put it: "I listened with great wonder to the Texas orators, as they talked about liberty. I thought that it might be as good for me as for others."[15]

Those who could not run away chose other forms of resistance. "They protested by shirking their duties, injuring the crops, feigning illness and disrupting the routine."[16] This has been called the "day-to-day resistance to slavery." Theft and arson were common also. Some slaves injured themselves by cutting off a finger or bruising an arm—deliberately unfitting themselves to work for masters. It was reported that "an Arkansas slave, 'at any time to save an hour's work,' could 'throw his left shoulder out of place.' "[17]

The prevalence of flight, theft, arson, and other forms of resistance meant that the slave and master did not share the same ethical perspective. Owners thought that "good" slaves were those who were obedient and diligent in the masters' interest, while the "bad" ones stole, malingered, or ran away. Black people rejected these definitions of good and bad, though they did not reject law and morality. Rather they formulated a *new* law and a *new* morality that reflected the requirements of *black* existence. Right and wrong were determined by *survival* needs in the context of servitude. To make ethical judgments in this context required that slaves "take the law into their own hands" and shape it into a useful instrument in the struggle for freedom. To be right meant doing whatever was necessary to stay alive with dignity. To be wrong meant accepting without struggle the place masters had defined for "niggers." The authentic ethical burden was the need to create one's own place, and "get in it" even though the risks were great.

An example was the ethical distinction between "stealing" and "taking." Stealing meant victimizing a fellow slave, and slave ethics did not condone that. But to take from white folks was not wrong because the slave was merely appropriating what in fact was rightfully his. "Don't say I'm wicked," said a defiant woman caught with some of her mistress' jewelry; "it's all right for us poor colored people to appropriate whatever of the white folks' blessing the Lord puts in our way."[18] It was good to take from whites whatever was necessary for black survival, comfort, or enjoyment.[19]

Another ingredient of slave ethics was deception. To survive in an oppressive society, it is necessary to outsmart the oppressors and make them think that you are what you *know* you are not. It is to make them believe that you accept their definitions of black and white. As one song puts it: "Got one mind for the boss to see; Got another mind for what I know is me."[20] To be able to deceive the master was often the only means of freedom, as when Lunsford Lane reported:

Even after I entertained the first idea of being free, I had endeavored so to conduct myself as not to become obnoxious to the white inhabitants, knowing as I did their power, and their hostility to the colored people The two points necessary in such a case I had kept constantly in mind. First, I had made no display of the little property or money I possessed, but in every way I wore as much as possible the aspect of slavery. Second, I had never appeared to be even so intelligent as I really was. This all colored people at the south, free and slaves, find it peculiarly necessary for their own comfort and safety to observe.[21]

Most masters read slave deception as reality and concluded that blacks were content. As one former Mississippian put it: "They find themselves first existing in this state, and pass through life without questioning the justice of their allotment, which, if they think at all, they suppose a natural one."[22] What he failed to understand was that the appearance of contentment was a tool of survival. When questioned, the slave would reply: "No massa, me no want to be free, have good massa, take care of me when I sick, never 'buse nigger; no, me no want to be free."[23] The reality of slave existence was brutal; a small assertion of one's humanity might result in death. The phrase "No, massa, me no want to be free" (despite the risk of believing it oneself and internalizing white values) was in fact an affirmation of a new kind of freedom. The slave knew that to say otherwise would involve possibilities he was not at the moment prepared to accept. Saying, "No, massa, me no want to be free," is a terrible experience, a pain, an event that has shaped the ethical experience of all blacks who have survived the white experience. "No, massa, me no want to be free" is both a depravity and a good. It is a depravity because we know that the statement is not what we are, and it never will be; but no one can *be* in the fullest sense of Blackness; therefore, the phrase "No massa, me no want to be free," can be a good, a means of survival. In an oppressive society it is necessary to deceive, to pretend "not-to-be," if an expression of being would destroy being. (Of course, sometimes authentic being is found only in not-being, but that can only be decided by the slave in the context of his community.) The polarity of being and not-being, of Yes and No, only means that slave existence is a risk and a search that never ends.

Resistance was the ability to create beauty and worth out of the ugliness of slave existence. *Resistance* made *dignity* more than just a word to be analyzed philosophically. Dignity was a reality that could only be dug out of the shit of the white environment; and it was based on the slaves' relationship with their black brothers and sisters. White people achieved what they called dignity by their enslavement of black Africans; they measured their importance by the number of Africans they enslaved. But what were the slaves to do? How could they assert their dignity, their humanity, and self-worth? They chose a life style that was defined by their group. The respected slave was the one who successfully challenged the rules of white society: "The strong-willed field-hand whom the overseer hesitated to punish, the habitual runaway who mastered the technique of escape and shrugged at the consequences, each won personal triumphs for himself and vicarious triumphs for the others."[24]

Related to the ethics of black resistance were the religious forms that slaves developed. Slaves were able to live a different ethical style than their masters because they constructed a different religion. Outwardly, the religion of the slaves seemed to be like the "Christian" religion as taught by the masters, but it was not. Religion is not a set of beliefs that people memorize and neither is it an ethical code of do's and don't's that they learn from others. Rather, religion is wrought out of the experience of the people who encounter the divine in the midst of historical realities. What the masters taught the slaves may have been consistent with the former's sociological expectations, but it had nothing to do with the condition of the slaves. Many slaves therefore merely pretended to accept white Christianity while actually holding quite different views.

The slaves were obliged to create their own religion out of the remnants that were available and useful, both African and Christian. These elements were woven together to provide a historical possibility for human existence. While white religion taught blacks to look for their reward in heaven through obedience to white masters on earth, black slaves were in fact carving out a new style of earthly freedom. Slave religion was permeated with the affirmation of freedom from bondage and freedom-in-bondage. Sometimes black religious gatherings were the occasions for planning overt resistance. At other times the reality of freedom was affirmed in more subtle ways. The theme of liberation that ran through slave religion explains why slaveholders did not allow black slaves to worship openly and sing their songs unless authorized white people were present to proctor the meeting. And after the Nat Turner revolt, black preachers were declared illegal in most southern states.[25]

It is the spirituals that show us the essence of black religion, that is, the experience of trying to be free in the midst of a "powerful lot of tribulation."

> Oh Freedom! Oh Freedom!
> Oh Freedom, I love thee!
> And before I'll be a slave,
> I'll be buried in my grave,
> And go home to my Lord and be free.

The spirituals are songs about black souls, "stretching out into the outskirts of God's eternity" and affirming that divine reality which lets you know that you are a human being—no matter what white people say. Through the song, black people were able to affirm that Spirit who was continuous with their existence as free beings; and they created a new style of religious worship. They shouted and they prayed; they preached and they sang, because *they had found something.* They encountered a new reality; a new God not enshrined in white churches and religious gatherings. And all along, white folk thought the slaves were contented, waiting for the next world. But in reality they were "stretching out" on God's Word, affirming a new-found experience that could not be destroyed by the masters. This is why they could sing:

> Don't be weary, traveller,
> Come along home, come home.
> Don't be weary, traveller,
> Come along home, come home.
>
> My head is wet with the midnight dew,
> Come along home, come home.
> The mornin' star was a witness too,
> Come along home, come home.
>
> Keep a-goin', traveller,
> Come along home, come home.

Keep a-singin' all the way,
Come along home, come home.

Jes' where to go I did not know,
Come along home, come home.
A trav'lin' long and a trav'lin' slow,
Come along home, come home.

The spirituals are historical songs which speak about the rupture of black lives; they tell us about a people in the land of bondage, and what they did to hold themselves together and to fight back. We are told that the people of Israel could not sing the Lord's song in a strange land. But, for blacks, their *being* depended upon a song. Through song they built new structures for existence in an alien land. The spirituals enabled blacks to retain a measure of African identity while living in the midst of American slavery, providing both the substance and the rhythm to cope with human servitude.

The Africanism in the spirituals is directly related to the *functional* character of African music.[26] In Africa and America, black music was not an artistic creation for its own sake; it was directly related to daily life, work and play. Song was an expression of the community's view of the world and its existence in it. Through music, Africans recorded their history, initiated the young into adulthood, and expressed their religious beliefs. When Africans were enslaved in America, they brought with them their culture as defined by their music. African culture provided the form that made it impossible for black slaves to accept a religion that negated their being as defined by their African heritage. In the spirituals, black slaves combined the memory of their fathers with the Christian gospel and created a style of existence that participated in their liberation from earthly bondage.

The spiritual, then, is the spirit of the people struggling to be free; it is their religion, their source of strength in a time of trouble. And if one does not know what trouble is, then the spiritual cannot be understood. This is what one black woman, who had lost all but one of her twenty-two children, meant when she said: "I likes 'Poor Rosy' better dan all de songs, but it can't be sung widout a *full heart and a troubled sperrit!*"[27] Trouble is inseparable from the black religious experience. For what is a people to do when they are "troubled in mind" and "they don't know where to roam"? What are they to do about the "end of tribulation," the "end of beatings and for shoes that fit their feet" when they are powerless economically and politically? The spiritual is the people's response to the societal contradictions. It is the people facing trouble and affirming, "I ain't tired yet."

But the spiritual is more than dealing with trouble. It is a joyful experience, a vibrant affirmation of life and its possibilities in an appropriate esthetic form. The spiritual is the community in rhythm, swinging to the movement of life. The best approach in interpreting the song is to *feel* one's way into the cultural and historical milieu of the people's mind and let the song speak *to* and *for* you. When the song is sung, "Have you got good religion?" and you can respond from the depths of the black soul, "Certainly Lord," then you are moving in the direction of the meaning of the spiritual. The meaning of the song is not contained in the bare words but in the black history that created it.

Black history then is the stuff out of which the black spirituals were created. But the "stuff" of black history includes more than the bare historical facts of slavery. Black history is an experience, a soulful event. And to understand it is to know the being of a people who had to "feel their way along the course of American slavery,"[28] enduring the stresses and strains of human servitude but not without a song. *Black history is a spiritual!*

In the chapters that follow we turn to examine the theological implications of black faith and experience, as expressed in the spirituals.

3

God and Jesus Christ in the Black Spirituals

We'll soon be free,
We'll soon be free,
We'll soon be free,
When de Lord will call us home.

The Meaning of God: God as Liberator

The divine *liberation* of the oppressed from slavery is the central theological concept in the black spirituals. These songs show that black slaves did not believe that human servitude was reconcilable with their African past and their knowledge of the Christian gospel. They did not believe that God created Africans to be the slaves of Americans. Accordingly they sang of a God who was involved in history—*their* history—making right what whites had made wrong. Just as God delivered the Children of Israel from Egyptian slavery, drowning Pharaoh and his army in the Red Sea, he will also deliver black people from American slavery. It is this certainty that informs the thought of the black spirituals, enabling black slaves to sing:

Oh Mary, don't you weep, don't you moan,
Oh Mary, don't you weep, don't you moan,

32

Pharaoh's army got drownded,
Oh Mary, don't you weep.

The basic idea of the spirituals is that slavery contradicts God; it is a denial of God's will. To be enslaved is to be declared *nobody*, and that form of existence contradicts God's creation of people to be God's children. Because black people believed that they were God's children, they affirmed their *somebodiness*, refusing to reconcile their servitude with divine revelation. They rejected white distortions of the gospel, which emphasized the obedience of slaves to their masters. They contended that God willed their freedom and not their slavery. That is why the spirituals focus on biblical passages that stress God's involvement in the liberation of oppressed people. Black people sang about Joshua and the battle of Jericho, Moses leading the Israelites from bondage, Daniel in the lions' den, and the Hebrew children in the fiery furnace. Here the emphasis was on God's liberation of the weak from the oppression of the strong, the lowly and downtrodden from the proud and mighty. And blacks reasoned that if God could lock the lion's jaw for Daniel and could cool the fire for the Hebrew children, then God could certainly deliver black people from slavery.

My Lord delivered Daniel,
My Lord delivered Daniel,
My Lord delivered Daniel,
Why can't He deliver me?

The message of liberation in the spirituals is based on the biblical contention that God's righteousness is revealed in deliverance of the oppressed from the shackles of human bondage. That message was an expression of the slave's confidence that God can be trusted to stand by God's word. God does not lie. The slave firmly believed that "God would make a way out of no way," meaning that God's providential care of God's children cannot be thwarted by white masters. So the slaves lived their life struggling to realize their human potentialities grounded in the faith that God's liberation is at work in the world; and God's will to liberate black slaves will become a reality in this land and "all flesh shall see it together." And they sang with assurance:

> Children, we shall be free
> When the Lord shall appear.
> Give ease to the sick, give sight to the blind,
> Enable the cripple to walk;
> He'll raise the dead from under the earth,
> And give them permission to talk.

The faith of black people was thus grounded in the authenticity of God's Word revealed through the scriptures.

This was precisely the quality of childlike trust that Jesus declared to be a precondition for entering the Kingdom of God. "Truly, I say to you, whoever does not receive the Kingdom of God like a child shall not enter it" (Luke 18:17). And according to the writer of Hebrews, "By faith Abraham obeyed when he was called to go out to a place ... not knowing where he was to go" (11:8). In each of these examples, the emphasis is upon faith in God's *Word of promise.* Israel left Egypt, made a covenant with God, and went into the Land of Canaan, and that was because Israel trusted God's Word of promise. There were no scientific evidences beforehand that gave the people assurance that they would not be overtaken by Pharaoh's army or that God would keep God's Word and ensure the people's safety to the land of promise. Indeed many Israelites complained continually to Moses about the risks of leaving Egypt. "For it would have been better for us to serve the Egyptians than to die in the wilderness." (Exodus 14:12). But Moses refused to be sidetracked by the people's fear of Pharaoh's approaching army, for he had already seen the burning bush and the mighty acts of God in God's contest with Pharaoh. "And Moses said to the people, 'Fear not, stand firm and see the salvation of the Lord, which he will work for you today; for the Egyptians whom you see today, you shall never see again' " (Exodus 14:13). Here we see that faith, as trust in God's Word of liberation, stands at the heart of biblical revelation. Israel is God's child; and even when Israel is disobedient, God will not reject her utterly. Israel left Egypt and entered Canaan because and only because God kept

God's Word, his promise to do for the people what they could not do for themselves. Similarly, black people trusted that their liberation depended upon God's action.

From this perspective there is nothing immature or demeaning about black folks having the humility and faith of children when they approach the throne of the Almighty. For it is only the proud and the mighty who think that they are the sole masters of their destiny and of everybody else's. This is the faith of white masters and overlords, and their pride keeps them from understanding why others do not want to be ruled by them. But the faith of black slaves is that people were created to be God's children, not someone else's slaves.

Faith in the righteousness of God was not easy for black people, since God's liberating work in the world was not always concretely evident. God did not always do *what* they wanted *when* they expected it. Their faith did not cancel the pain of enslavement. In the agony of faith and in the midst of suffering they sang

> Don't leave me,
> Lord Don't leave me behin'.

This plaintive cry was the equivalent of Israel's prayer-complaint, "How long, O Lord?" But despite the humiliation of servitude they rejoiced in God's constancy. God is a God who frees slaves: Israelites in Egypt, Africans in the United States.

> God is a God!
> God don't never change!
> God is a God
> An' He always will be God.

So far from being songs of passive resignation, the spirituals are black freedom songs which emphasize black liberation as consistent with divine revelation.[1] For this reason, it is most appropriate for black people to sing them in this "new" age of Black Power. And if some people still regard the spirituals as inconsistent with Black Power and Black Theology, that is because they have been misguided and the songs misinterpreted.

For enslaved blacks believed that there was an omnipotent, omnipresent, and omniscient power at work in the world who was on the side of the oppressed and downtrodden. As evidence they pointed to the blind man who received his sight, the lame who walked, and Lazarus who was received into God's kingdom while the rich man was rejected. And if "de God dat lived in Moses' time is jus de same today," then that God will vindicate the suffering of the righteous blacks and punish the unrighteous whites for their wrongdoings.

Some will argue, with Karl Marx, that the very insistence upon *divine* activity is always evidence that people are helpless and passive. "Religion is the sign of the oppressed creature, the heart of the heartless world . . . the spirit of a spiritless situation. It is the *opium* of the people."[2] There were doubtless some black slaves who *literally* waited on God, expecting God to effect their liberation in response to their faithful passivity; but there is another side of the black experience to be weighed. When it is considered that Nat Turner, Denmark Vesey, and Harriet Tubman may have been creators of some of the spirituals; that "Sinner, please don't let this harvest pass" probably referred to a slave resistance meeting;[3] that after 1831 over 2000 slaves escaped yearly;[4] and that black churches interpreted civil disobedience as consistent with religion; then it is clear that many slaves recognized the need for their own participation in God's liberation. Indeed many believed that the only hands God had were their hands and that without the hazards of escape or insurrection slavery would never end. This is implied in the song "Singin' wid a sword in ma han'," where the sword seems to be the symbol of the need of black slaves to strike a blow for freedom even though the odds were against them. Also, the spiritual "We die in the field" may be about an earthly struggle. The "Gospel War" and the "Journey Home" could be referring to the fight against masters and overseers in the struggle to be free. Certainly the strict enforcement of the slave codes and the merciless beatings of many slaves who sang spirituals at those secret meetings meant that whites thought black slaves had more on their minds than praising God.[5] But what we do know is that Christianity did not dull the drive for liberation among all black slaves, and there is much evidence that slaves appropriated the gospel to their various styles of resistance.

Against the foregoing interpretation, it has been contended that the theme of divine liberation from slavery was virtually absent from the slave songs. This contention has been supported by three assertions: (1) that the biblical literalism of the blacks forced them to accept the white prooftexts that implied God's approval of slavery; (2) that the black songs themselves were derived from white camp meeting songs and therefore reflected the *white* meaning of divine liberation as freeing one from sin, not slavery; and (3) that the spirituals do not contain "unequivocal references to the desire for freedom."[6]

1. In regard to biblical literalism it is of course true that slaves were not biblical critics and thus were unaware of European academic reflections on the origins of biblical writings emerging in response to the Enlightenment. Like most of their contemporaries, they accepted the inerrancy of scripture. But in contrast to white "fundamentalists" the black preachers have never been enslaved to the *words* of scripture. The texts of the Bible served as starting points for an interpretation consistent with the existence of the folk. James Weldon Johnson speaks of an occasion when a preacher "who after reading a rather cryptic passage took off his spectacles, closed the Bible with a bang and by way of preface said, 'Brothers and sisters, this morning—I intend to explain the unexplainable—find out the undefinable—ponder over the imponderable—and unscrew the unscrutable.' "[7] Now whatever may be said about that exegetically or theologically, this is not the style of a person enslaved to the literal words of scripture. He is a free person who is prepared to say whatever he believes necessary for the people. The Bible serves as a source for song and sermon ideas but not as an infallible authority equivalent with revelation itself. Revelation was distinctly historical and related to the event of the community encountering God in the struggle for freedom.

Traditionally, the black preacher was literal only about what he believed God would do for the people. The very literalism of black religion supported a gospel of earthly freedom. Black people were literal when they sang about Daniel in the lion's den,

David and Goliath, and Samson and the Philistines. On the other hand they dispensed with biblical literalism when white people began to use the curse of Ham and Paul as evidence that blacks ought to accept their slavery. As one ex-slave preacher put it:

> When I starts preaching I couldn't read or write and had to preach what Master told me, and he say tell them niggers iffen they obeys the master they goes to Heaven; but I knowed there's something better for them, but daren't tell them 'cept on the sly. That I done lots. I tells 'em iffen they keeps praying, the Lord will set 'em free.[8]

Black slaves were not so naive as is often supposed. They knew that slavery contradicted humanity and divinity, and that was why they cited biblical references that focused on the liberation of the oppressed. They believed that God would deliver them; and as God locked the lion's jaw for Daniel, God would paralyze the power of white masters.

> Who lock, who lock de lion,
> Who lock, de lion's jaw?
> God, lock, God lock de lion's jaw.

The point is clear. God is the liberator, the deliverer of the weak from the injustice of the strong.

2. The argument about the influence of white camp meeting songs upon the black spirituals contains a measure of truth. Such influence was doubtless present. However, there were other powerful influences upon the black songs that enabled them to become vehicles of a distinctively Black Theology. One of these sources was African culture. Melville Herskovits and Miles Fisher argue persuasively that elements of African culture were present in the United States in the nineteenth century. Considering that large numbers of Africans were imported as late as 1807 it would be surprising if African influence were not present in the theology of the spirituals. If that datum is taken seriously, then there is reason to believe that freedom in the slave songs

has a decisive *historical* referent. Africans viewed life as a *whole* and did not make the distinctions between the "secular" and the "sacred" that are found in Western culture. With this perspective as a starting point, it is reasonable to conclude that African slaves could not and did not accept a religion that negated historical freedom. As I suggested earlier, they combined their African heritage with the Christian gospel and reinterpreted white distortions of the gospel in the light of oppressed people striving for a historical liberation.

The second distinctively black source of the spirituals was the slave experience itself. When asked where black people got their songs, one slave responded: "Dey make 'em, sah." He paused and was requested to continue:

> I'll tell you; it's dis way. My master call me up and order me a short peck of corn and a hundred lash. My friends see it and is sorry for me. When dey come to de praise meetin' dat night dey sing about it. Some's very good singers and know how; and dey work it in, work it in, you know; till dey get it right; and dat's de way.[9]

According to Thomas Wentworth Higginson, an oarsman gave a similar account of origin:

> Once we boys . . . went for tote some rice and de nigger-driver he keep a-callin' on us; and I say, "O, de ole nigger-driver!" Den anudder said, "Fust ting my mammy tole me was, notin' so bad as nigger-driver." Den I made a sing, just puttin' a word, and then anudder word.[10]

In view of these reports, it is no surprise to find the slaves singing about "rollin' through an unfriendly worl'," laying down their heavy load, and telling God about their troubles.

> I don't know what my mother wants to stay here fuh,
> Dis ole worl' ain't been no friend to huh.

It was not "sin" but the pain and suffering of slavery that made up the problem of black people.

O I been rebuked, and I been scorned,
Done had a hard time sho's you born.

It is not likely that songs so concretely related to the oppression of slavery would revert to abstraction or metaphor when speaking of freedom. As Sterling Brown summarizes the case:

Free, individualistic whites on the make in a prospering civilization, nursing the American dream, could well have felt their only bondage to be that of sin, and freedom to be religious salvation. But with the drudgery, the hardships, the auction-block, the slave mart, the shackles, and the lash so literally present in the Negro's experience, it is hard to imagine why for the Negro they would remain figurative.[11]

Both the African heritage and the slave experience guaranteed that the black spirituals would not be imprisoned by white definitions of God's liberating work.

3. Concerning the claim that the songs do not speak unequivocally of freedom, it must be pointed out that there was good reason for equivocation. Slaves lived in a society without any political, economic, or personal security, and they had to camouflage their deepest feelings. White song collectors heard what the slave permitted them to hear, and there is some evidence that many songs were reserved only for the ears of fellow slaves. For example, Higginson reported that blacks stopped singing on one occasion when he appeared. "My presence apparently checked the performance of another verse," wrote Higginson, "beginning 'De buckra' list for money.' " The slave knew that a too obvious reference of a condemnation of whites or a slight reference to political freedom in the presence of white people could mean his or her life. But despite the risks, there were some fairly obvious references to historical freedom. And one does not have to be too bright to detect something more than "spiritual" freedom in such spirituals as:

O freedom! O freedom!
O freedom over me!

An' befo' I'd be a slave,
I'll be buried in my grave,
An' go home to my Lord an' be free.

My Lord delivered Daniel,
Why can't he deliver me?

When Israel was in Egypt's land,
Let my people go;
Oppressed so hard they could not stand,
Let my people go;
Go down, Moses, 'way down in Egypt's land;
Tell ole Pharaoh
Let my people go.

My contention that the pre-Civil War songs (although ambiguous) did in fact refer to earthly freedom is supported by the
fact that black people made unequivocal statements as soon as
the need for equivocation was removed. These are the songs
that blacks sang in response to the Civil War and Emancipation.

There may have been many historical and sociological causes
of the freedom of black slaves; but blacks viewed it as an act of
God in history analogous to Israel's exodus from Egypt. Abraham Lincoln's decision to engage in war and issue the Emancipation Proclamation was seen as God's way of making justice
a reality for black slaves on earth. That is why they lifted their
voices to God in song:

Slavery chain done broke at last, broke
     at last, broke at last,
Slavery chain done broke at last,
Going to praise God till I die.

Way down in-a dat valley,
Praying on my knees;
Told God about my troubles,
And to help me ef-a He please.

I did tell him how I suffer,
In de dungeon and de chain,

And de days I went with head bowed down,
And my broken flesh and pain.

I did know my Jesus heard me,
'Cause de spirit spoke to me,
And said, "Rise my child, your chillun,
And you shall be free.

"I done 'p'int one mighty captain
For to marshall all my hosts,
And to bring my bleeding ones to me,
And not one shall be lost."

Slavery chain done broke at last, broke
     at last, broke at last,
Slavery chain done broke at last,
Going to praise God till I die.

For black people, the end of slavery was God's liberating act on behalf of oppressed people. As one ex-slave expressed it:

I 'members 'bout the days of slavery, and I don't 'lieve they ever gwine have slaves no more on this earth. I think God done took that burden offen his black children, and I'm aiming to praise Him for it to His face in the days of glory which ain't far off.[12]

This is not a "spiritual" freedom; it is an eschatological freedom grounded in the events of the historical present, affirming that even now God's future is inconsistent with the realities of slavery.

Freedom, for black slaves, was not a theological idea about being delivered from the oppression of sin. It was a historical reality that had transcendent implications. Freedom meant the end of "driber's dribin'," "Massa's hollerin'," and "missus' scoldin' " — "Roll, Jordan, roll." It meant that there would be "no more peck o' corn," "no more driver's lash," "no more pint o' salt," "no more hundred lash," and "no more mistress's call for me, Many thousand gone."

Freedom at last!
Freedom at last!
Great God-a-mighty,
Freedom at last!

The slaves' view of God embraced the whole of life—their joys and hopes, their sorrows and disappointments; and their basic belief was that God had not left them alone, and that God would set them free from human bondage. That is the central theological idea in black slave religion as reflected in the spirituals.

The Meaning of God: Jesus Christ

It is significant that theology proper blends imperceptibly into Christology in the spirituals. That is, statements about God are not theologically distinct from statements about Jesus Christ. Jesus is understood as the King, the deliverer of humanity from unjust suffering. He is the comforter in time of trouble, "the lily of the valley," and "the bright and morning star."

He's King of Kings, and Lord of Lords,
Jesus Christ, the first and the last
No man works like him.

The spirituals are silent on abstract theological speculations about the person and work of Christ. There are no theories about the *ousia* or Being of the Son in relation to the Father. (It is safe to assume that black slaves did not know about the proceedings at Nicea and Chalcedon.) Jesus was not the subject of theological questioning. He was perceived in the reality of the black experience, and black slaves affirmed both his *divinity* and *humanity* without debating the philosophical question, "How can God become human being?"

The divinity of Jesus was affirmed unequivocally in the black spirituals. Language about the Father and the Son became two ways of talking about the reality of divine presence in the slave community. They stood for that reality who enabled black people to transcend the strict limitations of slavery. The choice of name (Father or Son) often depended largely upon the rhythm of the language in which people expressed their desire to be free, rather than upon the intellectual content of the language.

> De Father he look upon de Son an' smile,
> De Son he look upon me,
> De Father redeemed my soul from hell,
> De Son he set me free.

It was as if black slaves were affirming their freedom through the rhythm, the passion, and the motion of their language. If the words did not sound right, feel right, and move smoothly from the lips, then how could they be an expression of the soul's yearning for freedom? Freedom was the mind and body in motion, emotionally and rhythmically asserting the right to be. Language could not describe that reality unless it too was liberated to become what the people felt was consistent with the soul's yearning for being. "Jesus" then was not a thought in their heads to be analyzed in relation to a related thought called "God." Jesus was an experience, a historical presence in motion, liberating and moving the people in freedom. When black slaves encountered his presence, they also met the Father who sent the Son to give his people liberty.

> I'm a chile of God wid my soul set free,
> For Christ hab bought my liberty.

Although the Son is divine, he is also human. He was born of "Sister Mary" in Bethlehem, and "everytime the baby cried, she'd a-rocked Him in the weary land." The spirituals tell us of Jesus' life on earth, and of his rejection and death on the cross. There is no suggestion of a docetic or gnostic Christ who only appeared to be human. His suffering was real and his pain was great. He died the death of a natural man.

According to the spirituals, the meaning of Jesus' birth, life, death, and resurrection is found in his identity with the poor, the blind, and the sick. He has come to set them free, to restore their wholeness. He is the conquering King and the crucified

Lord who has come to bring peace and justice to the dispos-
sessed of the land. That was why the slaves wanted to

> Go tell it on de mountain,
> Over de hills and everywhere,
> Go tell it on de mountain,
> That Jesus Christ is born.

The birth of Jesus meant that "de Savior's born"; that was why
the "Three Wise Men to Jerusalem Came" and why the shep-
herds were commanded to "rise up . . . an' foller."

> Leave yo' sheep an' leave yo' lambs,
>   Rise up, shepherd, an' foller.
> Leave yo' ewes an' leave yo' rams,
>   Rise up, shepherd, an' foller.

To follow meant accepting the significance of his birth and what
that meant for the unimportant people in the society. Through
him the poor have the good news preached to them, but the rich
and the rulers will be condemned to everlasting punishment.
That was why

> King Herod's heart was troubled,
> He marvelled but his face was grim.

There was much that could have been said about the birth of
Jesus and the birth of black slaves. Each was born in "out-of-
the-way places" because there was no room for them in the
society. But the curious fact is the spirituals are almost silent
regarding the birth of Jesus. Their silence has given rise to much
speculation. James Weldon Johnson has given three possibilities,
one of which is particularly convincing: "The reason may he due
in part to the fact that the anniversary of the birth of Christ was
not, in the South, in any sense a sacred or religious holiday."[13]
Christmas was a time of whiskey, gunpowder, singing, dancing,
and visiting. "It is possible that it was a conscious part of the
scheme of slavery to make Christmas a day on which slaves
through sheer excess of sensuous pleasure would forget their

bonds.''[14] This is similar to Howard Thurman's contention that
the white masters, overseers, and preachers intentionally overlooked the birth of Christ because of its significance for the
political liberation of the oppressed. "In the teachings of the
Bible stories concerning the birth of Jesus, very little appeal was
made to the imagination of the slave because it was not felt wise
to teach him the significance of this event to the poor and the
captive. It was dangerous to let the slave understand that the
life and teachings of Jesus meant freedom for the captive and
release for those held in economic, social, and political bondage.''[15]

In contrast to the nativity of Christ his life, death, and resurrection are particular focal points of the spirituals. Jesus is
pictured as the Oppressed One who could "make de dumb to
speak," "de cripple walk," and "give de blind his sight." "Jesus
do most anything." Because of the miraculous power of the
Savior, the slaves pleaded for Jesus to be with them.

> Be with me Lord! Be with me!
> Be with me Lord! Be with me!
> When I'm on my lonesome journey,
> I want Jesus Be with me.
>
> When I'm in trouble, Be with me!
> When I'm in trouble, Be with me!
> When I'm on my lonesome journey,
> I want Jesus Be with me.
>
> When I'm dying, Be with me!
> When I'm dying, Be with me!
> When I'm on my lonesome journey,
> I want Jesus Be with me.

Slaves wanted Jesus to be with them so the savior could help
them make it to the Kingdom and not fall prey to the troubles
of this world. They knew of Jesus' presence with Peter: "Peter
walked upon the sea because Jesus told him, 'Come to me.'"
They had heard about "King Jesus preaching to the poor," heal-
ing the lame, and giving sight to the blind. Black people con-

cluded that that same "Jesus Christ, He died for me, Jesus Christ, He set me free." Therefore, they pleaded, "Come here Jesus if you please." Slaves wanted Jesus to do for them what he had done for others.

> O Lord, I'm hungry
> I want to be fed,
> O Lord, I'm hungry
> I want to be fed,
> O feed me Jesus feed me,
> Feed me all my days.

> O Lord, I'm naked
> I want to be clothed,
> O Lord, I'm naked
> I want to be clothed,
> O clothe me Jesus clothe me,
> Clothe me all my days.

> O Lord, I'm sinful
> I want to be saved,
> O Lord, I'm sinful
> I want to be saved,
> O save me Jesus save me
> Save me all my days.

Black folks believed that Jesus could save them from the oppression of slavery because of his death and resurrection. They were deeply moved by the Passion story because they too had been rejected, beaten, and shot without a chance to say a word in defense of their humanity. In Jesus' death black slaves saw themselves, and they unleashed their imagination, describing what they felt and saw.

> Oh, dey whupped him up de hill, up de hill, up de
>   hill,
> Oh, dey whupped him up de hill, an' he never said
>   a mumbalin' word,

Oh, dey whupped him up de hill, an' he never said
    a mumbalin' word,
He jes' hung down his head an' he cried.

Oh, dey crowned him wid a thorny crown, thorny
    crown, crown o' thorns,
Oh, dey crowned him wid a thorny crown, an' he
    never said a mumbalin' word,
Oh, dey crowned him wid a thorny crown, an' he
    never said a mumbalin' word,
He jes' hung down his head an' he cried.

Well, dey nailed him to de cross, to de cross, to de
    cross,
Well, dey nailed him to de cross, an' he never said a
    mumbalin' word,
Well, dey nailed him to de cross, an he never said a
    mumbalin' word,
He jes' hung down his head an' he cried.

Well, dey pierced him in de side, in de side, in de
    side,
Well, dey pierced him in de side, an' he never said
    a mumbalin' word,
Well, dey pierced him in de side, an' he never said
    a mumbalin' word,
Den he hung down his head an' he cried.

Well, de blood came twinklin' down, twinklin' down,
    twinklin' down,
Well, de blood came twinklin' down, an' he never
    said a mumbalin' word,
Well, de blood came twinklin' down, an' he never
    said a mumbalin' word,
Den he hung down his head an' he died.

The death of Jesus meant that he died on the cross for black
slaves. His death was a symbol of their suffering, trials, and

tribulations in an unfriendly world. They knew the agony of rejection and the pain of hanging from a tree.

> They nail my Jesus down,
> They put him on the crown of thorns,
> O see my Jesus hangin' high!
> He look so pale an' bleed so free:
> O don't you think it was a shame,
> He hung three hours in dreadful pain?

Because black slaves knew the significance of the pain and shame of Jesus' death on the cross, they found themselves by his side.

> Were you there when they crucified my Lord?
>   Were you there when they crucified my Lord?
> Oh! sometimes it causes me to tremble, tremble,
>   tremble;
>   Were you there when they crucified my Lord?

> Were you there when they nailed Him to the tree?

> Were you there when they pierced Him in the side?

> Were you there when He bowed His head and died?

Through the blood of slavery, black slaves transcended the limitations of space and time. Jesus' time became their time, and they encountered a new historical existence. Through the experience of being slaves, they encountered the theological significance of Jesus' death: through the crucifixion, Jesus makes an unqualified identification with the poor and the helpless and takes their pain upon himself.

If Jesus was not alone in his suffering, black slaves were not alone in their oppression under slavery. Jesus was with them! He was God's Black Slave who had come to put an end to human bondage. Herein lies the meaning of the resurrection. It means that the cross was not the end of God's drama of salvation.

Death does not have the last word. Through Jesus' death, God has conquered death's power over his people.

> He arose, he arose from the dead,
> An' de Lord shall bear my spirit hom'.

The resurrection is the divine guarantee that black people's lives are in the hands of the Conqueror of death, and now they are free to do what is necessary to remain obedient to God, the creator and sustainer of life. They don't have to cry anymore.

> Weep no more, Marta,
> Weep no more, Mary,
> Jesus rise from de dead,
> Happy Morning.

> Glorious morning,
> Glorious morning,
> My Savior rise from de dead,
> Happy Morning.

The resurrection was an eschatological event which permeated both the present and future history of black slaves. On the one hand, Jesus was present[16] in that he was their friend and companion in slavery. He enabled the people to bear the trouble and endure the pain of loneliness in oppression.

> Jesus is our friend,
> He'll keep us to the en'
> And a little talk with Jesus,
> Makes it right.

Jesus was their "rock in a weary lan'," their "shelter in a time of storm"; he was the one whom the slaves could tell all about their trials. They could write to him, and when the burdens became too much for them to bear, they would take them to the Lord in prayer.

> Sometimes I hangs my head an' cries,
> But Jesus goin' to wipe my weep'n eyes.

Christ is the ever-present help in trouble, "O, Jesus is a mighty man."

> He pluck my feet out'n de miry clay,
> He set dem on de firm rock of ages.

But there was another meaning to the resurrection of Jesus. Black slaves also looked beyond the present to the future of Jesus, and they saw the Lord high and lifted up. The spirituals speak not only of what Jesus has done and is doing for blacks in slavery. Jesus was understood as holding the keys to Judgment, and therefore the full consummation of God's salvation will take place outside of the historical sphere. Jesus is the Son of God who dwells in heaven. And he is coming again; but this time "he ain't coming to die." He is coming to complete God's will to set free "the poor, black, and wasted." He will take them home to be with him.

> I'm going back with Jesus when He comes, when He
>   comes,
> I'm going back with Jesus when He comes, when He
>   comes,
> O He may not come today,
> But He's coming anyway
> I'm going back with Jesus when He comes, when He
>   comes.

> And we won't die anymore when He comes, when
>   He comes,
> And we won't die anymore when He comes, when
>   He comes,
> O He may not come today,
> But He's coming anyway
> And we won't die anymore when He comes, when
>   He comes.

> And He's going to bring my mother with Him when
>   He comes, when He comes,

> And He's going to bring my mother with Him when
>   He comes, when He comes,
> O He may not come today
> But He's coming anyway
> And He's going to bring my mother with Him when
>   He comes, when He comes.

Because the black slave was confident that God's eschatological liberation would be fully revealed in Jesus' Second Coming, he could sing songs of joy and happiness while living in bondage. He played and laughed about religious matters.

> Why don't you sit down?
> Can't sit down!
> Sit down, I told you!
> I can't sit down.
> Go 'way don't bother me,
> I can't sit down
> 'Cause I just got to heaven
> An' I can't sit down!

The black person was certain that God's ultimate future would usher in a radically different reality that would end slavery.

> When I gets to heaven, gonna be at ease,
> Me an' my God gonna do as we please.

For black slaves, Jesus is God breaking into their historical present and transforming it according to divine expectations. Because of the revelation of Christ, there is no need to worry about the reality of liberation. It is already at hand in Jesus' own person and work, and it will be fully consummated in God's own ordained future.

4

God and Black Suffering

Oh, Lord, Oh, My Lord!
Oh, My Good Lord!
Keep me fo'm sinkin' down.

Although black slaves believed that the God of Jesus Christ was involved in the historical liberation of oppressed people from bondage, the continued existence of American slavery seemed to contradict that belief. If God is omnipotent and is in control of human history, how can God's goodness be reconciled with human servitude? If God has the power to deliver black people from the evil of slavery as God delivered Moses from Pharaoh's army, Daniel from the lion's den, and the Hebrew children from the fiery furnace, why then are black slaves still subject to the rule of white masters? Why are we still living in wretched conditions when God could end this evil thing with one righteous stroke?

These are hard questions, and they are still relevant today. In the history of theology and philosophy, these questions are the core of the "problem of evil"; and college and seminary professors have spent many hours debating them. But black slaves did not have the opportunity to investigate the problem of suffering in the luxury of a seminar room with all the comforts of modern living. They encountered suffering in the cotton fields of Georgia, Arkansas, and Mississippi. They had to deal with the absurdities of human existence under whip and pistol. Every time they opened their eyes and visualized the contradictions of their environment, they realized that they were "rolling through an unfriendly world." How could a good and powerful God be reconciled with white masters and overseers? What explanation could the Holy One of Israel give for allowing the existence of an ungodly slave institution?

Faith and Suffering in the Bible

In order to understand the black slaves' reaction to their enslavement, it is necessary to point out that their reflections on the problem of suffering were not "rational" in the classical Greek sense, with its emphasis on abstract and universal distinctions between good and evil, justice and injustice. The black slaves had little time for reading books or sitting in the cool of the day, thinking about neat philosophical answers to the problem of evil. It was not only illegal to teach slaves to read, but most were forced to work from daybreak to nightfall, leaving no spare time for the art of theological and philosophical discourse. The black slaves' investigation of the absurdities of human existence was concrete, and it was done within the context of the community of faith. No attempt was made to transcend the faith of the community by assuming a universal stance common to "all" people. In this sense, black reflections on human suffering were not unlike the biblical view of God's activity in human history. It was grounded in the historical realities of communal experience.

The classic examples in biblical literature are found in the books of Habakkuk the prophet and of Job. In both, questions are raised about the justice of God, but they were clearly questions for the faithful, not for philosophers. They had significance only for members of the community of faith. Habakkuk was concerned about the cruelty of Assyrian oppression against Judah and also about the internal corruption of Judah under the inept rule of Jehoiakim. Why was God silent and inactive as the wicked oppressed the righteous?

Oh Lord, how long shall I cry for help,
    and thou wilt not hear?

Or cry to the "Violence!"
    and thou wilt not save?
Why dost thou make me see wrongs
    and look upon trouble?

Destruction and violence are before me;
    strife and contention arise.
So the law is slacked
    and justice never goes forth.
For the wicked surround the righteous,
    so justice goes forth perverted.
                                    (1:2-4)

And God's contention that God is "rousing the Chaldeans" (1:
6) to put down the wicked Assyrians does not really satisfy the
prophet, even though he recognizes that the Lord "hast
ordained them as a judgment; and thou, O Rock, hast established them for chastisement" (1:12). The issue is *justice*! How
can the Holy One of Israel justify the use of wicked and faithless
men as the instrument of divine righteousness?

Thou who art of purer eyes than to behold evil
    and canst not look on wrong,
Why dost thou look on faithless men,
    and art silent when the wicked swallows up
    the man more righteous than he?
                                    (1:13)

If God is righteous and is in control of history, why is God not
setting things right?
    The author of the book of Job had a similar concern about
the justice of God. Writing probably during the Exile (sixth century B.C.E.), he protested against the deuteronomic doctrine of
retribution, according to which God rewards people according
to their obedience and punishes them in proportion to their
disobedience. The author contended that not all suffering is on
account of disobedience; for although Job was "blameless and
upright, one who feared God, and turned away from evil" (1:1),
he suffered severe mental and physical anguish. If the deuter-

onomic success formula is true, then God is a demon and does not know righteousness.

Both Habakkuk and Job are concerned about the faithfulness of the people who are condemned to live in the midst of injustice and suffering. How can the people depend upon God, when so much historical evidence seems to point toward God's being either an evildoer or uninterested in the fate of the people? Is faith in God possible when the righteousness of God seems to be absent in everyday affairs? Neither Job nor Habakkuk questioned the ultimate sovereignty of God. What was requested was a divine explanation of God's righteousness in history so that the faithful could understand the ways of the Almighty.

The "answer" came, not in thought but in *encounter*. There was no philosophical resolution to the problem of evil. Both Job and Habakkuk recognized that suffering was a reality of life. But they wanted to know: "How can the believer live in pain without losing faith in God?" Habakkuk and Job received God's answer in the form of divine self-disclosure.

> And the Lord answered me:
> "Write the vision;
>   make it plain upon tablets,
>   so he may run who reads it.
> For still the vision awaits its time;
>   it hastens to the end—it will not lie.
> If it seem slow, wait for it;
>   it will surely come, it will not delay.
> Behold, he whose soul is not upright in him shall fail,
>   but the righteous shall live by his faith."
> (Habakkuk 2:2-4)

And Job says, after the disclosure of God's mighty presence: "I had heard of thee by the hearing of the ear, but now my eye sees thee" (42:5).

Because the faithful can experience the reality of divine presence, they can endure suffering and transform it into an event of redemption. An encounter with God is the ultimate answer to the question of faith, and it comes only in and through the struggle for righteousness—not in passivity.

Black Faith and Suffering

The black slaves' response to the experience of suffering corresponded closely to the biblical message and its emphasis that God is the ultimate answer to the question of faith. In the spirituals, the black slaves' experience of suffering and despair defined for them the major issue in their view of the world. They do not really question the justice and goodness of God. It was taken for granted that God is righteous and will vindicate the poor and the weak. Indeed it was the point of departure for faith. The singers of spirituals had another concern, centered on the *faithfulness* of the community of believers in a world full of trouble. They wondered not whether God is just and right but whether the sadness and pain of the world would cause them to lose faith in the gospel of God. They were concerned about the solidarity of the community of sufferers. Will the wretched of the earth be able to experience the harsh realities of despair and loneliness and take this pain upon themselves and not lose faith in the faithfulness of God? There was no attempt to evade the reality of suffering. Black slaves faced the reality of the world "ladened wid trouble, an' burden'd wid grief," but they believed that they could go to Jesus in secret and get relief. They appealed to Jesus not so much to remove the trouble (though that was included), but to keep them from "sinkin' down."

> Oh, Lord, Oh, My Lord!
> Oh, My Good Lord! Keep me fom sinkin' down.
> Oh, Lord, Oh, My Lord!
> Oh, My Good Lord! Keep me fom sinkin' down.

Significantly, the note of despair was usually intertwined with confidence and joy that "trouble don't last always." To be sure, the slaves sang "Sometimes I feel like a motherless child, A long way from home"; but because they were confident that Jesus was with them and had not left them completely alone, they could still add (in the same song!), "Glory Hallelujah!" The same conjunction also occurred in:

Nobody knows the trouble I've seen
Nobody knows my sorrow.
Nobody knows the trouble I've seen,
Glory, Hallelujah!

The "Glory, Hallelujah!" was not a denial of trouble; it was an affirmation of faith: God is the companion of sufferers, and *trouble* is not the last word on human existence. This was why they could sing with assurance:

Soon-a-will be done with the trouble of the world;
Soon-a-will be done with the trouble of the world;
Going home to live with God.

Or again, they sang:

All-a-my troubles will soon be over with,
All-a-my troubles will soon be over with,
All over this world.

It appears that slaves were not troubled by the problem of evil in its academic guise; they knew intuitively that nothing would be solved through a debate on that problem. They dealt with the world as it was, not as it might have been if God had acted "justly." They attended to the present realities of despair and loneliness that disrupted the community of faith. The faithful seemed to have lost faith, and the brother or sister experienced the agony of being alone in a world of hardship and pain.

I couldn't hear nobody pray,
Oh, I couldn't hear nobody pray.
Oh, way down yonder by myself,
And I couldn't hear nobody pray.

Thus it is the loss of community that constitutes the major burden. Suffering is not too much to bear, if there are brothers and sisters to go down in the valley to pray with you.

O brothers let's go down, let's go down, let's go down,
O brothers let's go down, down in the valley to pray.

O sisters let's go down, let's go down, let's go down,
O sisters let's go down, down in the valley to pray.

O children let's go down, let's go down, let's go down,
O children let's go down, down in the valley to pray.

By-an'-by we'll all go down, all go down, all go down,
By-an'-by we'll all go down, down in the valley to
pray.

The actual physical brutalities of slavery were minor in comparison to the loss of the community. That was why most of the slave songs focused on "going home." Home was an affirmation of the need for community. It was the place where mother, father, sister, and brother had gone. To be sure, the slaves wanted to make it to heaven so they could put on their "golden slippers and walk all over God's heaven"; they wanted to see the "pearly gates" and the "golden streets"; and they wanted to "chatter with the Father, argue with the Son" and "tell um 'bout the world [hc] just come from." But most of all, they wanted to be reunited with their families which had been broken and scattered in the slave marts.

I'm just a-goin' 'way over Jordan
I'm just a-goin' over there,
I'm goin' home to see my brother,
I'm just a-goin' over there.

I'm just a-goin' 'way over Jordan
I'm just a-goin' over there,
I'm goin' home to see my mother,
I'm just a-goin' over there.

In the midst of a broken community, slaves might wonder whether existence had any meaning at all without mother, father, brother, or sister.

If I had-a my way,
If I had-a my way, little children,

> If I had-a my way,
> I'd tear this building down.
> Great God, then, if I had-a my way,
> If I had-a my way, little children,
> If I had-a my way,
> I'd tear this building down.

Nevertheless, despite the brokenness of community and family inflicted by slavery, slaves continued to hold on doggedly to what life and existence they had. The affirmation of life, as expressed in their strivings for being, was possible because they believed that they were sheltered in the care of the Lord. They "remembered" the Exodus, the Covenant, the prophets; and, most of all, Jesus' life, death, and resurrection. Through the remembrance of these events, they encountered God, and they realized that they were not (as an old prayer says) "put here for any ship-shape form nor fashion, nor for any outside show to this unfriendly world." God the Creator and Jesus Christ the Savior have included them in the plan of salvation, and it does not matter *ultimately* what wicked men do with mama and papa, sister and brother. The authentic community of saints is bound up with the encounter of God in the midst of a broken existence, struggling to be free. God is the Community! And all earthly communities must be evaluated in the light of the divine presence. To those who know God in their strivings for being, God is a mother to the motherless, a father to the fatherless. "He is a very present help in trouble"—and much more. God is the Liberator of black people and gives them a victory that is not made with human hands.

However, slaves realized that the victory which God gives is not cheap. The journey of salvation is like a lonesome valley with hard trials, and the believer has to travel the valley for herself.

> I must walk my lonesome valley
> I got to walk it for myself,
> Nobody else can walk it for me,
> I got to walk it for myself.

I must go and stand my trial,
I got to stand it for myself,
Nobody else can stand it for me,
I got to stand it for myself.

Jesus walked his lonesome valley,
He had to walk it for himself,
Nobody else could walk it for him,
He had to walk it for himself.

It is commonplace among many interpreters of black religion to account for the emphasis on the "I" in the spirituals and other black church expressions by pointing to the influence of white pietism and revivalism in the nineteenth century.[1] But that assumption, while having some merit, is too simplistic; it does not take seriously enough the uniqueness of black religion. Black people did not unquestioningly adopt the white interpretation of scriptural language. Rather, they invested scriptural language with the meaning that was consistent with their struggle to affirm themselves as people, their identity and their freedom. The existential "I" in black religion, then, did not have as its content the religious individualism and guilt of white religion or refer to personal conversion in those terms. Neither was it simply a black duplication of the Protestant idea of the priesthood of all believers. The "I" of black slave religion was born in the context of the brokenness of black existence. It was an affirmation of self in a situation where the decision to *be* was thrust upon the slaves. But the slaves did not determine the historical setting in which they had to make this affirmation; it had been determined by others against them. And so to affirm their being meant that their existence had to be managed in that inimical setting. That was the situation of blacks who found themselves slaves in "the land of the free." The "I," then, who cries out in the spirituals is a particular black self affirming both his or her being and being-in-community, for the two are inseparable. Thus the struggle to be both a person and a member of community was the major focus of black religion. The slaves knew that an essential part of this struggle was to maintain this affirmation even and especially when alone and separated from the community and its support. They knew that they alone were accountable to God, because somewhere in the depth of the soul's search for meaning, they met the divine. The revelation from that encounter made it plain to them that the divine and human are bound inseparably together. When black slaves suffered, God suffered. Evil was not just their problem; it was God's problem too. That was why they could not believe that God willed his slavery. In the agony of this contradiction, the slaves cried for deliverance:

> O wretched man that I am
> O wretched man that I am
> O wretched man that I am,
> O who will deliver po' me.
>
> I'm bowed down with a burden of woe
> I'm bowed down with a burden of woe
> I'm bowed down with a burden of woe,
> O who will deliver po' me.

In this context one may wonder why there were no direct attacks upon God in the spirituals, like those found in Habakkuk and Job? If slaves really believed that God was in control of history, why were they silent about the apparent divine neglect to end slavery? There are at least two responses. In the first place, not all slaves were silent. There is evidence of open rebellion against God; some of it is found in another style of black music that is almost as old as the spirituals. These songs are commonly called slave "seculars," and today they are known as the *blues*. More will be said in Chapter 6 about the significance of the "seculars." Here we simply note the evidence that not all slaves accepted an unquestioning faith in God. Sterling Brown reports that blacks sang: "I don't want to ride no golden chariot; I don't want no golden crown; I want to stay down here and be, just as I am without one plea." " 'Live a humble to the Lord' was changed to 'Live a humbug.' " And they also sang:

> Our father, who is in heaven,
> White man owe me eleven and pay me seven,

Thy kingdom come, thy will be done,
And if I hadn't took that, I wouldn't had none.[2]

Daniel Payne (elected Bishop of the African Methodist Episcopal Church in 1852) reported that many slaves denied the existence of God because they could not reconcile divine revelation with human servitude.

The slaves are sensible of the oppression exercised by their masters; and they see these masters on the Lord's day worshipping in his holy Sanctuary. They hear their masters professing Christianity; they see their masters preaching the gospel; they hear these masters praying in their families, and they know that oppression and slavery are inconsistent with the Christian religion; therefore they scoff at religion itself—mock their masters, and distrust both the goodness and justice of God. Yes, I have known them even to question his existence. I speak not of what others have told me, but of what *I have both seen and heard from the slaves themselves.* I have heard the mistress ring the bell for family prayer, and I have seen the servants immediately begin to sneer and laugh; and have heard them declare they would not go in to prayers; adding if I go in she will not only just read, "Servants obey your master;" but she will not read "break every yoke, and let the oppressed go free." I have seen colored men at the church door, scoffing *at the ministers*, while they were preaching, and saying, you had better go home, and set your slaves free. A few nights ago . . . a runaway slave came to the house where I live for safety, and succor. I asked him if he were a Christian; "no sir," said he, "white men treat us so bad in Mississippi that we can't be Christians."[3]

Payne also reported his own personal difficulties in reconciling the justice of God with human slavery.

I began to question the existence of the Almighty, and to say, if indeed there is a God, does he deal justly? Is he a just God? Is he a holy Being? If so, why does he permit a handful of dying men thus to oppress us? . . . Thus I began to question the Divine government, and to murmur at the administration of his providence. And could I do otherwise, while slavery's cruelties were pressing and grinding my soul in the dust, and robbing me and my people of these privileges which it was hugging to its breast, and giving thousands to perpetuate the blessing which it was tearing away from us?[4]

Other black preachers had similar difficulties, and they protested not just to whites or to blacks, but to God. They demanded, in words similar to Habakkuk and Job, that God give an account of God's sovereignty. Nathaniel Paul made it plain:

Tell me, ye mighty waters, why did ye sustain the ponderous load of misery? Or speak, ye winds, and say why it was that ye executed your office to waft them onward to the still more dismal state; and ye proud waves, why did you refuse to lend your aid and to have overwhelmed them with your billows? . . . And, oh thou immaculate God, be not angry with us, while we come into this thy sanctuary, and make the bold inquiry in this thy holy temple, why it was that thou didst look on with the calm indifference of an unconcerned spectator when thy holy law was violated, thy divine authority despised and a portion of thine own creatures reduced to a state of mere vassalage and misery?[5]

These are difficult theological questions, and they belong to the biblical tradition that took seriously the righteousness and goodness of God. Like Job and Habakkuk, Nathaniel Paul did not receive a philosophical answer. He did not ask a philosophical question! It was a question of faith, and the answer which came focused on *revelation* as the only clue to historical absurdities.

Hark! while he answers from on high: hear Him proclaiming from the skies—Be still, and know that I am God! Clouds and darkness are round about me; yet righteousness and judgment are the habitation of my throne. I do my will and pleasure in the heavens above, and in the earth beneath; it is my sovereign prerogative to bring good out of evil, and cause the wrath of man to praise me, and the remainder of that wrath I will restrain.[6]

In the second place, there was a good reason for the measure of restraint shown in the spirituals. They do not make direct attacks upon God, because questions about God's justice did not represent a major religious problem for black slaves. The spirituals are not songs of protest against God because black slaves did not perceive the source of their oppressed condition as being ordained by God or Jesus Christ.

Sociology of knowledge and its emphasis on the relation between ideas and the social condition of the people expounding them is worth remembering here. The social and cultural environment of the people determine the kinds of religious questions they ask. This is not to deny that revelation provides its own questions or has its own integrity (a concern that dominated Karl Barth's theological works). But the integrity of revelation must be encountered to the human situation. The situation of being an American slave created certain kinds of theological problems, but they were not the same theological problems of white slave masters or others who did not live out their lives as slaves. Therefore, to use European or Western theological and philosophical methodologies as a means of evaluating the significance of black reflections on the slave condition is not only theoretically inappropriate but very naive. To evaluate correctly the slaves' theological reflection on their servitude in relation to divine justice, it is necessary to suspend the methodology of the enslavers and to enter the cultural and religious milieu of the victims. What were the theological questions of the *slave* community? What were the assumptions that defined the movement of *that* community?

The theological assumption of black slave religion as expressed in the spirituals was that *slavery contradicts God*, and *God will therefore liberate black people*. All else was secondary and complemented that basic perspective. But how did black slaves *know* that God was liberating them? Black slaves did not ask that epistemological question. As with all faith assumptions, the *truth* of a theological assertion is found in the givenness of existence itself and not in theory. Black slaves did not devise philosophical and theological methodologies in order to test the truth of God's revelation as liberation. From their viewpoint it did not need testing. They had already encountered its truth and had been liberated by it. Instead of testing God, they *ritualized* God in song and sermon. That was what the spirituals were all about—a ritualization of God in song. They are not documents for philosophy; they are material for worship and praise to the One who had continued to be present with black humanity despite European insanity.

According to Ernst Bloch, "need is the mother of thought." In other words, reflective thought directly relates to perceived wants. Bloch's observation can be very helpful to us at this point in understanding the prominence of certain themes in the spirituals and, conversely, the absence of others. The spirituals nowhere raise questions about God's existence or matters of theodicy, and it is safe to assume that the slave community did not perceive a theoretical solution of the problem of evil as a felt need. Rather, their needs were defined by the existential realities which they encountered. As slaves, they felt sharply their oppression and complete lack of freedom. In the Bible, the black slaves found the God who liberated the Israelites from bondage and whose will was the liberation of the oppressed. This same God also came to humanity in Jesus Christ the Oppressed One, who disclosed that God's will from all eternity was not to be reconciled with human slavery. Moreover, the death and resurrection of Jesus made clear God's will to deliver the oppressed. This biblical disclosure the slaves appropriated as speaking directly to their own condition. Whether they reasoned correctly about the Bible's message is irrelevant, a question for speculative discussion by those not entrapped in their situation.

That this theme of God's involvement in history and the liberation of the oppressed from bondage should be central in black slave religion and the spirituals is not surprising, for it corresponded with the black people's need to know that their slavery was not the divine Creator's intention for them. In fastening on this knowledge, they experienced the awareness of divine liberation. Their experience of it and their faith in its complete fulfillment became factual reality and self-evident truth for the slave community. Only those outside the community and the experience could dare question it or remain unconvinced. To be sure, they did not deny:

> Sometimes I'm up, sometimes I'm down,
> Oh, yes, Lord!
> Sometimes I'm almost to the ground,
> Oh, yes, Lord!

But the certain fact is always that God is present with them and trouble will not have the last word. Penultimately, white masters may torture and kill slaves capriciously, and the world seem only chaos and absurdity. But ultimately God is in control and black slaves believed that they had encountered the infinite significance of God's liberation. And so they lifted up their voices and sang:

> Do, Lord, remember me.
> Do, Lord, remember me.
> When I'm in trouble,
> Do, Lord, remember me.
>
> When I'm low down,
> Do, Lord, remember me.
> Oh, when I'm low down,
> Do, Lord, remember me.

The Meaning of Death

Related to the problem of suffering was the fact of death. Death is the symbol of nothingness, and the possibility of the complete annihilation of being. Black slaves feared death because they regarded it as the opposite of life and therefore evil. Accordingly, much of their energy was expended in just trying to *be* and in avoiding the encompassing power of nonbeing. And that was not easy in nineteenth-century America. The central question for black slaves was: How can we survive, and still retain a measure of our personhood, that essential human ingredient without which we cannot *be*?

The difficulty was that of drawing the line between dignity and nothingness. In a slave society where blacks were regarded as property, how were they to balance the scale between being and nonbeing, life and death? Black slaves knew that any *open* assertion of their being would be regarded as a threat by slave masters, who were virtually outside the law and could make decisions of life and death even on whim. Thus black people were well acquainted with death, for they lived under its threat every moment. The slave owners, in particular, and white people generally, were vivid reminders that life could not be taken for granted. It had to be defended all the time by all possible means. To stay alive in dignity was the essential task of the black slave community.

Black slaves ritualized in song this constant presence of death and the threat of death.

> Soon one mornin', death comes a-creepin' in my
> room.
> O my Lawd, O my Lawd, what shall I do?

Death had already visited the slave quarters leaving orphans behind.

> Death done been here, tuck my mother an' gone,
> O my Lawd, what shall I do?

> Death done been here, left me a motherless child,
> O my Lawd, O my Lawd, what shall I do?

Death then was not an abstract idea or an unknown force. The black slaves' "contact with the dead was immediate, inescapable, dramatic."[7] They kept watch over the dying, prepared the corpse, made the grave clothes, built the coffin, and dug the grave. Because the reality of death was a part of their everyday experience, blacks spoke of it in personal terms. Death was "a little ole man" who "came tippin' in the room," "a man goin' round takin' names," and "a robber."

Death ain't nothin' but a robber, don't you see.
Death ain't nothin' but a robber, don't you see.

Death came to my house, he didn't stay long,
I looked in the bed an' my mother was gone,
Death ain't nothin' but a robber, don't you see.

Death came to my house, he didn't stay long
I looked in the bed an' my father was gone,
Death ain't nothin' but a robber, don't you see.

Death came to my house, he didn't stay long,
I looked in the bed an' my brother was gone,
Death ain't nothin' but a robber, don't you see.

Death was also "a hammer ringin' on a coffin," "a pale horse an' a rider," "a chariot swingin' low," and "a train a-blowin' at de station."

Same train, same train,
Same train carry my mother,
Same train be back tomorrow;
Same train, same train.

Same train, carry my sister,
Same train be back tomorrow;
Same train, same train.

Same train blowin' at the station,
Same train be back tomorrow;
Same train, same train.

Then again, death was a decisive moment of time: when, "all in my room, gonna hear the angels singin' "; when "if I got my ticket, I'm gonna ride"; when "I'm gonna put on my wings and try the air"; when "one cold freezing morning I lay dis body down."[8]

Black slaves accepted the inevitability of death. They knew

that the "train was coming along" and that death was "goin' to lay his cold icy hands on [them]."

> Before this time another year,
> I may be gone;
> Out in some lonely graveyard,
> O Lord, how long?

But because of Jesus' death and resurrection, black slaves did not believe that death was ultimate. It was inevitable and perhaps a dreadful experience, but it did not have the last word.

> When I get to heav'n I will sing and tell,
> How I did shun both death and hell.

Black slaves believed that Christ had defeated death on the cross and had assured the faithful that they would be received into his Kingdom. Therefore, death was sometimes interpreted as a welcome release from the burdens of this world.

> You needn't mind my dying,
> You needn't mind my dying,
> You needn't mind my dying,
> Jesus goin' to make up my dying bed.

> In my dying room I know,
> Somebody is going to cry.
> All I ask you to do for me,
> Just close my dying eyes.

> In my dying room I know,
> Somebody is going to mourn.
> All I ask you to do for me,
> Just give that bell a tone.

For black slaves, Christ was the fixed point of certainty in a world of uncertainties, contradictions, and death. He bestowed upon the people a status of being, enabling them to transcend death. They could therefore accept death and ask their loved ones not to weep.

> When I'm gone,
> When I'm gone,
> When I'm gone, gone, gone,
> Mother, don't you weep when I am gone.
>
> For I'm goin' to Heav'n above,
> Going to meet the God I love,
> O mother, don't you weep when I am gone.

Black people only made the request that they be allowed to die like Jesus died.

> I want to die easy when I die.
> I want to die easy when I die.
>   Shout salvation as I fly,
> I want to die easy when I die.
>
> I want to die like-a Jesus die,
>   And he died wid a free good will,
> I lay out in the grave and stretched out my arms,
>   Do, Lord, remember me.

To die easy and with a free good will meant that blacks would be accepted into the Kingdom and that they could become what God wanted them to be. It meant that they had "left their burdens at the river and in the valley." Evil was no longer a problem.

> You can't hurt me!
> For I'm sheltered!
> In my Jesus!

The Meaning of Satan

Like the concept of death, the idea of Satan is also prominent in the spirituals, although it is not always obvious what is meant by references to Satan. According to Howard Odum and Guy B. Johnson, Satan represented "the demon trickster incarnate in the form of a man. He is the opposite of God but always less powerful."[9] He is the evil that is responsible for the sinfulness of human beings. In this interpretation, Satan is a "spiritual" demon but not really related to the social structures of slavery. In contrast, John Lovell interprets Satan in the spirituals in the light of the social setting of slavery.[10] Satan is the one who hinders the fight for black political freedom. Specifically, he is the slaveholders, the slave traders, the drivers, the overseers. Both views have some merit. The weakness of Odum and Johnson's view stems from their failure to account for that form of slave religion which included liberation from the social, political, and economic conditions of slavery. Lovell, on the other hand, tends to overlook the significance of theological language as a means of interpreting the sociality of the slave's existence.

To explicate adequately the concept of Satan in the spirituals we need to recall the New Testament's understanding of the role of principalities and powers. In the New Testament Satan is the adversary of God and of all who belong to him. Satan is the slanderer, "the prince of the demons" (Matthew 12:24; Luke 11:15), and the Evil One (or Evil personified). Christ's ministry was a battle against Satan, and the conflict began with his temptation in the wilderness and reached its climax with his death on the cross. However, the war between God and Satan did not end there. Battles continue to be fought in concrete human events. Satan is not merely an abstract metaphysical evil unrelated to social and political affairs; he represents the concrete presence of evil in human society. That was why exorcisms were central in the ministry of Jesus. The casting out of demons was an attack upon Satan because Jesus was setting people's minds free for the Kingdom which was present in his ministry. To be free from Satan meant to be free for Jesus, who was God making liberation a historical reality. Anyone who was not for the Kingdom, as present in the liberating work of Jesus, was automatically for Satan, who stood for enslavement.

Black slaves took the biblical description of Satan as the Evil One and applied it to their experience. Satan for them was a supernatural being who enslaved people in sin. Though less powerful than God, Satan was more powerful than people. And blacks believed that "if you ain't got the grace of God in yo' heart, den de dehbil will git you sho." Satan controls the kingdom of hell and seeks to convince people to follow him and not Jesus Christ. However, Satan is not only a cosmic seducer but is present in the concrete world of human oppression. Like God who came and is present in Jesus Christ, Satan also makes his presence known in history. Just as God is present in the forces that make people human and enable them to struggle against the evils of slavery, so Satan is present in the dehumanizing forces that contribute to slavery. Satan's earthly representatives are slaveholders, slave catchers, and slave traders.

> Ole Satan like dat hunting dog,
> He hunt dem Christians home to God.

> Ole Satan thought he had me fas';
> Broke his chain an' I'm free at las'.

Although Satan is alive and concrete, he is no contest against the powers of God. In the New Testament and the spirituals, Satan is fighting a losing battle.

> Go 'way, Satan, I doan min' you;
> You wonder, too, you can't come through?

> I plucked one block out o' Satan's wall,
> I heard him stumble an' saw him fall.

The slaves felt assured that they would make it through, and neither death, Satan, nor white people could prevent God from effecting the liberation of black people from bondage.

> The devil tries to throw down everything that's good,
> He'd fix a way to confuse the righteous if he could,
> Thanks be to God-er mighty, he can't be beguiled,
> Old Satan will be done fighting after awhile.

The Meaning of Sin

No interpretation of suffering would be complete without an analysis of sin. According to the spirituals, black slaves believed that they were fighting not only against death and Satan but also against sin. What is sin, and how is it related to the black slaves' attempt to achieve authentic personhood?

1. Sin is related to death and Satan. To deny Christ is to accept Satan; and to follow Satan is to live according to sin which can only lead to death and eternal damnation.

> O the gift of God is eternal life,
> O the gift of God is eternal life,
> And the wages of sin is death.

Blacks believed that Satan was responsible for the presence of sin in the world. He was the embodiment of sin, the "Sinner Man" personified. Eternal death in hell was the consequence of sin.

2. While sin is related to death and Satan, it is not identical with either concept. Sin is also a universal concept that defines the human condition as separation from God. If God is known as the liberator of the oppressed from bondage, and Jesus is God's Son who is still present today, then the "Sinner Man" is everyone who is in need of divine liberation. He is the person who needs "dat ol' time religion" or the one "standin' in the need of prayer."

> It's me, it's me,
> It's me, O Lord,
> Standin' in the need of prayer.
>
> Tain't my mother or my father,
> But it's me, O Lord,
> Standin' in the need of prayer.

Sin is that concept that expresses human alienation from God. It means that the creature is not what the Creator intends. The "Sinner Man" then is the one for whom Christ died in order to set him free.

> Sinner, please, don't let dis harves' pass,
> An' die, an' lose yo' soul at las'.
>
> Sinner, O, see dat cruel tree,
> Where Christ has died for you an' for me.

Through Jesus Christ's death and resurrection, the power of sin was conquered. Satan was defeated and thus no one has to fear death anymore. People are now free to live according to God's manifestation of his active liberation in the present and his promise of ultimate liberation in the future. This truth was expressed in song: "The Lord's been here and blessed my soul" and "I ain't goin' lay my religion down."

The expression of joy and gladness in the spirituals is directly related to the black slaves' experience of divine liberation from this "sin-trying world" and the bondage of Satan.

> Old Satan's mad and I am glad,
> That's what Satan's a-grumbling about,
> He missed that soul he thought he had,
> That's what Satan's a-grumbling about.

3. The concept of sin was also used to refer to persons who disregarded the saving event of Jesus on the cross. The "Sinner Man" was the disobedient brother or sister who failed to come out of the "wilderness" and receive the grace of God.

> O poor sinner,
> O now is your time,
> O poor sinner,
> O What you goin' to do
>   when your lamp burns down?

Here the emphasis was placed on willful disobedience in the presence of the Word of God that offered salvation. How is it

possible to hear the Word of freedom in song, sermon, and
historical events and still refuse to live according to the liberating presence of Christ? Why is it that some have already "seen
the light" and joined that "gospel band" while others refuse to
let "Jesus wash [their] sins away"?

> Yonder comes my brother,
> Whom I loved so well,
> But by his disobedience,
> Has made his home in hell.

4. Despite the clear implication that the white system of slavery is *generally* Satanic, there is a surprising absence of references to white people as a *special* object of hate and scorn. One
would expect indirect expressions of resentment, if not direct
references. But aside from such songs as "Everybody talking
about heaven, ain't going there" and "When I get to Heaven,
goin' to sing and shout, there will be nobody there to turn me
out," the spirituals are strangely silent on the ethical behavior
of the white masters. Most of them focus on the ethical respon-
sibilities of members within the black community. Some critics
have used this as evidence that black slaves accepted their slave
condition but it has already been shown that such an explanation
is hardly probable. Howard Thurman's explanation is closer to
the truth. He contends that the slaves had been so ruthlessly
treated as things by white masters that blacks soon learned to
expect nothing but evil from white people. "The fact was that
the slave owner was regarded as one outside the pale of moral
and ethical responsibility. . . . Nothing could be expected from
him but gross evil—he was in terms of morality—amoral."[11] It
was as if the slaves regarded white people as natural phenom-
ena, like tornadoes, earthquakes, or floods. For whites had dem-
onstrated that they had no feeling or compassion for suffering
humanity, and many slaves considered it unwise to deal with
them on moral, human grounds.

If the spirituals had addressed the ethical behavior of whites,
the slaves would have been assuming that white people were
human and thus had the moral capability of listening to their
protest. Protest assumes community—that the victim of injustice

is a brother, a sister, a friend. There was nothing in the experience of black slaves in their relation to white people that could have supported that assumption. Black slaves expected nothing. White people are, after all, Satan's representatives on earth and you don't make deals with devils. The responsibility of Christians is to strive against evil.

5

The Meaning of Heaven
in the Black Spirituals

I am a poor pilgrim of sorrow. I'm in this world alone. No hope in this world for tomorrow. I'm trying to make heaven my home.

Related to the experience of suffering and death was the problem of the future, the "last things," which in theology is called eschatology. How was it possible for black slaves to take seriously their pain and suffering in an unfriendly world and *still* believe that God was liberating them from earthly bondage? How could they *really* believe that God was just when they knew only injustice, oppression, and death? What exactly was revealed in their encounter with God that made them know that their humanity was protected from the insanity of white masters and governmental officials? The answer to these questions lies in the concept of heaven, which is the dominant idea in black religious experience as expressed in the black spirituals.

As I have suggested in previous discussion, the concept of heaven in black religion has not been interpreted rightly. Most observers have defined the black religious experience exclusively in terms of slaves longing for heaven, as if that desire was unrelated to their earthly liberation. It has been said that the concept of heaven served as an opiate for black slaves, making for docility and submission. It may be that part of this charge is related to the outmoded cosmology of the spirituals. Their old-fashioned "world pictures" can blind modern critics to the message of a people seeking expression amid the dehumanization of slavery. It is like discarding the Bible and its message as irrelevant because the biblical writers had a three-storied conception of the universe. While not all biblical and systematic theologians agree with Rudolf Bultmann's method of "demythologization" as the way to solve the problem (among others) of biblical cosmology, most would agree that he is correct in his insistence that the gospel message is not invalidated by its prescientific world-picture. A similar perspective can illumine the heaven theme in the spirituals.

Let me admit then that the black slaves' picture of the world is not to be defended as a viable scientific analysis of reality; that the language of heaven was a white concept given to black slaves in order to make them obedient and submissive; that the image of the Promised Land, where "the streets are pearl and the gates are gold," is not the best one for communicating with contemporary Black Power advocates, who stress political liberation by any means necessary; that a "new" black theological language is needed if black religion is going to articulate today the historical struggles of black people in America and the Third World. The question nevertheless remains: How was it possible for black people to endure the mental and physical stresses of slavery and still keep their humanity intact? I think the answer is found in the image of heaven. Maybe what is needed is not its dismissal but a reinterpretation, so that oppressed blacks today can develop styles of resistance not unlike those of their grandparents.

Heaven and Black Existence

The place to begin is with Miles Fisher's contention that the spirituals are primarily "historical documents." They tell us about the black movement for historical liberation, the attempt of black people to define their present history in the light of their promised future and not according to their past miseries. Fisher notes that heaven for early black slaves referred not only to a transcendent reality beyond time and space; it designated the earthly places that blacks regarded as lands of freedom. Heaven referred to Africa, Canada, and the northern United States.[1]

Frederick Douglass wrote about the double meanings of these songs:

> We were at times remarkably buoyant, singing hymns, and making joyous exclamations, almost as triumphant in their tone as if we had reached a land of freedom and safety. A keen observer might have detected in our repeated singing of "O Canaan, sweet Canaan, I am bound for the land of Canaan," something more than a hope of reaching heaven. We meant to reach the *North*, and the *North* was our Canaan.[2]

Harriet Tubman also used the spirituals in her struggle to free black people from the bonds of slavery. The spirituals were communicative devices about the possibilities of earthly freedom. Sarah Bradford[3] reported how Tubman used the song in order to let her relatives and friends know that she intended to escape North to freedom.

When dat ar ole chariot comes,
    I'm gwine to lebe you,
I'm boun' for de promised land,
    Frien's, I'm gwine to lebe you.

I'm sorry, frien's, to lebe you,
    Farewell! oh, farewell!
But I'll meet you in de mornin',
    Farewell! oh, farewell!

I'll meet you in de mornin',
    When you reach de promised land;
On de oder side of Jordan,
    For I'm boun' for de promised land.

As with Douglass, Tubman's concept of "de promised land on de oder side of Jordan" was not just a transcendent reality. It was the North and later Canada. Said Harriet, after reaching free territory: "I looked at my hands to see if I was de same person now I was free. Dere was such a glory ober everything, de sun came like gold trou de trees, and ober de fields, and I felt like I was in heaven."[4]

However, she was not content to be free while others remained in bondage.

> I had crossed de line of which I had so long been dreaming. I was free; but dere was, no one to welcome me to de land of freedom, I was a stranger in a strange land, and my home after all was down in de old cabin quarter, wid de ole folks, and my brudders and sisters. But to dis solemn resolution I came; I was free, and dey should be free also; I would make a home for dem in de North, and de Lord helping me, I would bring dem all dere. Oh, how I prayed den, lying all alone on de cold, damp ground; "Oh, dear Lord," I said, "I hain't got no friend but you. Come to my help, Lord, for I'm in trouble!"[5]

According to Sarah Bradford, Harriet went back South nineteen times and brought with her "over three hundred pieces of living and breathing "property"[6] to the promised land.

In this context "Swing Low, Sweet Chariot" referred to the "idea of escape by 'chariot,' that is, by means which a company could employ to proceed northward." When black slaves sang, "I looked over Jordan and what did I see, Coming for to carry me home," they were looking over the Ohio River. "The band of angels was Harriet or another conductor coming for him; and 'home' was a haven in the free states or Canada."[7] "Steal away" meant to sneak into the woods for a secret slave meeting, and "Follow the Drinking Gourd" meant following the Great Dipper to the Ohio River and freedom.[8]

But while it is true that heaven had its this-worldly topographical referents, not all black slaves could hope to make it to Africa, Canada, or even to the northern section of the United States. The ambiguity and failure of the American Colonization Society's experiments crushed the hopes of many black slaves who were expecting to return to their African homeland. And blacks also began to realize that the North was not so significantly different from the South as they had envisioned, particularly in view of the Fugitive Slave Act of 1850 and the Dred Scott Decision in 1858. Black slaves began to realize that their historical freedom could not be assured as long as white racists controlled the governmental processes of the United States. Thus they found it necessary to develop a style of freedom that *included* but *did not depend upon* historical possibilities. What could freedom mean for black slaves who could never expect to participate in the determination of the laws governing their lives? Must they continue to define freedom in terms of the possibility of escape and insurrection, as if their humanity depended on their willingness to commit suicide? It was in response to this situation that the black concept of heaven developed.

For black slaves, who were condemned to carve out their existence in captivity, heaven meant that the eternal God had made a decision about their humanity that could not be destroyed by white masters. Whites could drive them, beat them, and even kill them; but they believed that God nevertheless had chosen black slaves as God's own and that this election bestowed upon them a freedom to be, which could not be measured by what oppressors could do to the physical body. Whites may suppress black history and define Africans as savages, but the words of slave masters do not have to be taken seriously when the oppressed know that they have a *somebodiness* that is guaranteed by God who alone is the ultimate sovereign of the universe. This is what heaven meant for black slaves.

The idea of heaven provided ways for black people to affirm their humanity when other people were attempting to define them as non-persons. It enabled blacks to say yes to their right to be free by affirming God's promise to the oppressed of the freedom to be. That was what they meant when they sang about a "city called heaven."

> I am a poor pilgrim of sorrow.
> I'm in this world alone.
> No hope in this world for tomorrow.
> I'm trying to make heaven my home.

Sometimes I am tossed and driven.
Sometimes I don't know where to roam.
I've heard of a city called heaven.
I've started to make it my home.

My mother's gone on to pure glory.
My father's still walking in sin.
My sisters and brothers won't own me
Because I'm tryin' to get in.

In the midst of economic and political disfranchisement, black slaves held themselves together and did not lose their spiritual composure, because they believed that their worth transcended governmental decisions. That was why they looked forward to "walking in Jerusalem just like John" and longed for the "camp meeting in the promised land."

It is evident that the pre-scientific images of heaven in these songs point to a biblical emphasis usually glossed over by New Testament scholars. Black slaves are expressing the Christian contention that the death and resurrection of Christ bestows upon people a freedom that cannot be taken away by oppressors. They were saying: "We are human beings and not even the slave masters can do anything about that!"

The Transcendent Present

Even where there is no overt or hidden reference to specific historical events, the spirituals employ eschatological language to express transcendence in the slaves' present existence. "I've *started* to make heaven my home," "Marching up the heavenly road, I'm bound to fight till I die" — such lines make clear that black slaves were not passively waiting for the future; they were actively living as if the future were already present in their community.

O glory, glory, hallelujah!
  O glory, glory to that Lamb;
O glory, glory, hallelujah!
  Child of God, that's what I am!

To be a child of God had present implications. It meant that God's future had broken into the slave's historical present, revealing that God had defeated evil in Jesus' crucifixion and resurrection. The black slave could experience *now* a foretaste of that freedom which is to be fully revealed in the future. That was what the writer of I John had in mind when he wrote: "We are God's children now" (3:2). The future had become present in the resurrection of Jesus and no one had to be a slave anymore. A slave's personhood or "soul" was free to be what was consistent with God's act of liberation.

> One day, one day, while walkin' along,
>   Jesus done bless my soul;
> I heard a voice an' saw no one,
>   Jesus done bless my soul.
> O go an' tell it on de mountain,
>   Jesus done bless my soul;
> O go an' tell it in de valley,
>   Jesus done bless my soul.
> He done bless my soul an' gone to glory, Good Lord,
>   Jesus done bless my soul;
> Done bin here an' bless my soul an' gone on to glory,
>   Jesus done bless my soul.

Again, in a similar fashion, the slave described the realized dimensions of God's eschatological presence.

> One day when I was walkin' alone, Oh yes, Lord,
> De element opened, an' de Love came down, Oh yes,
>   Lord,
> I never shall forget dat day, Oh yes, Lord,
> When Jesus washed my sins away, Oh yes, Lord.

These songs make clear that the future is not simply a reality to come. It is a reality that has already happened in Jesus' resurrection, and is present now in the midst of the black struggle for liberation. To accept the future of God as disclosed in the present means that we cannot be content with the present political order. God's eschatological presence arouses discontent-

ment and makes the present subject to radical change. That was
why black slaves could not "sit down." They were on the move,
"tryin' to get home." They accepted the consequences of the
eschatological Kingdom, and opened their minds and hearts to
the movement of the future. They were bound for the Kingdom
that was breaking into the already new present, and they
affirmed their willingness to "git on board" that "gospel train."

> Git on board, little chillen,
> Git on board, little chillen,
> Git on board, little chillen,
> Dere's room for many a mo'.
>
> De gospel train's a-comin',
> I hear it jus' at han',
> I hear de car wheels movin',
> An' rumblin' thro de lan'.
>
> De fare is cheap, an' all can go,
> De rich an' poor are dere,
> No second class a-board dis train,
> No difference in de fare.
>
> Git on board, little chillen,
> Git on board, little chillen,
> Git on board, little chillen,
> Dere's room for many a mo'.

The only requirement for acceptance on the "gospel train"
was the willingness to *move*, to step into the future. Those who
were bound to the present by earthly possessions would not
likely give up everything and accept the risk of the future. But
black slaves did not have that problem since their present meant
only slavery. They could "step on board" because they had nothing to lose and everything to gain. The "gospel train" meant the
possibility of freedom.

Because black slaves believed that the gospel was a message
about the future of God, breaking into the reality of their present, they were liberated *from* the bondage of the present and

free to be *for* God's future. In this sense, the partly revealed future of God, as disclosed in the cross and resurrection of Christ, made black people resist the condition of enslavement. Indeed, if the Kingdom was truly present in their midst, and if it was really ultimate, then they *had* to disobey all values that hindered their obedience to the coming Kingdom. Heaven then did not mean passivity but revolution against the present order. Against overwhelming odds, black people fought the structures of slavery and affirmed their membership in a "city whose builder and maker was God."

In the black spirituals, the image of heaven served functionally to liberate the black mind from the existing values of white society, enabling black slaves to think their own thoughts and do their own things. For Tubman and Douglass, heaven meant the risk of escape to the North and Canada; for Nat Turner, it was a vision from above that broke into the minds of believers, giving them the courage and the power to take up arms against slave masters and mistresses. And for others, heaven was a perspective on the present, a spiritual, a song about "another world . . . not made with hands." It was a black life-style, a movement and a beat to the rhythm of freedom in the souls and bodies of black slaves. It was a hum, a moan, and a hope for freedom. Blacks were able, through song, to transcend the enslavement of the present and to live as if the future had already come.

Hope, in the black spirituals, is not a denial of history. Black hope accepts history, but believes that the historical is in motion, moving toward a divine fulfillment. It is the belief that things can be radically otherwise than they are: that reality is not fixed, but is moving in the direction of human liberation.

> There is a balm in Gilead,
> To make the spirit whole.
> There is a balm in Gilead,
> To heal the sin-sick soul.

To believe that there was hope in the midst of oppression meant that black slaves' vision of the future was not limited to their present state of slavery. They looked beyond the condition of servitude and perceived that the real meaning of their existence was still to come. The absurd present was not eternal, and they were free to change it according to their vision of the future. As Howard Thurman put it: "It is an optimism that uses the pessimism of life as raw material out of which it creates its own strength."[9]

The present moment of slavery was thus transcended by faith in God's future, a liberated future. The divine future broke into their wretchedness. They seized God's future, the Word of God's promise, as the strength for carving out a future for themselves. They had also to seize the future from white masters and overlords who were continuing to deny them any future other than that of chattel to be sold on the auction block in slave marts.

To create the future in the "extreme situation" of American slavery was very difficult for black slaves. It meant accepting the burden and the risk of the "not yet." Actually, when they encountered the divine presence and promise, as revealed in the event of Jesus' death and resurrection, they knew that there was only *one* possibility for authentic human existence. And that was to *live* in *freedom* for the *future*. They said what they said and did what they did not because of any "logic" in the physical reality that encompassed them—where could they find an empowering logic in the situation of their servitude?—but because they intuitively understood the necessity to affirm life, to respond to life. In this sense they did not "choose" their future; it was thrust upon them as the only divine possibility reconcilable with their humanity. This all-important affirmation rested not on an epistemological base, but on a faith base that allowed them no other response.

The Transcendent Future

The concept of heaven was not exhausted by historical reality or present existence. It expressed something besides the capacity of black people to be human in the midst of suffering and despair. In the spirituals, heaven was also hope in the future of God, an expectation that the contradictions of slavery were not ultimate. They believed that life did not end with death and that somewhere in the "bosom of God's eternity," God would rectify the wrongs against black people. "We are God's children now; it does not yet appear what we shall be, *but we know that when he appears we shall be like him, for we shall see him as he is*" (I John 3:2). The "not yet" affirmed the *novum* of divine presence that was still to come. It was the expectation of the future of God, grounded in the resurrection of Jesus, that was the central theological focus of the black religious experience. This hope in a radically new future, defined solely by God the Liberator, was expressed in the spirituals in two ways: (1) language about heaven as a different sort of *place* after death and (2) language about the "last days," a new kind of *time*.

   1. Heaven was a place where the oppressed would "lay down dat heavy load" as mother and father had done before. It was a place where slaves would put on their robes, take up their harps, and put on their shoes and wings. It was "dat Rock," the slaves' true home, the Promised Land down by the riverside. "In dat great gettin' up mornin'," the oppressed of the land would be received into a "New Jerusalem."

> I want to go to heaven when I die,
> To shout salvation as I fly.
>
> You say yer aiming fer de skies,
> Why don't yer quit tellin' lies?
>
> I hope I git dere by an' by,
> To mine de number in de sky.
>
> We'll walk up an' down dem golden streets,
> We'll walk about Zion.
>
> When I get to heaven goin' set right down,
> Gwin-er ask my Lord for starry crown.
> Now wait till I gits my gospel shoes,
> Gwin-er walk 'bout heaven an' carry de news.

   Heaven was the place for the mourner, the despised, the rejected, and the black.

My Lord! Po' mourner's got a home at las'.
Mourner's got a home at las'.

O, Mourner, mourner,
Ain't you tired o' mournin',
Bow down on-a yo' knees an'
Join de ban' wid de angels.

O, No harm, Lord, no harm,
Go tell brudder Elijah,
No harm, Lord, No harm,
Po' mourner's got a home at las'.

It was a home indeed, where slaves would sit down by Jesus, eat at the welcome table, sing and shout, because there would be nobody there to turn them out. The black slave took seriously Jesus' promise in the Fourth Gospel that he would prepare a place for them, a place with many mansions (14:2, 3).

In bright mansions above,
In bright mansions above,
Lord, I want to live up yonder;
In bright mansions above.

The "mansions above" were God's Kingdom, a heavenly place of rest and peace from the pain of slavery.

No more hard trial in de kingdom; no more tribulation, no more parting, no more quarreling, back-
biting in de kingdom,
No more sunshine fer to bu'n you no more rain fer
to wet you.
Every day will be Sunday in heaven.

Heaven was God's eschatological promise; it was a place of "golden streets," "pearly gates," and "the long white robes." There would be no more sadness, no more sorrow and no more hunger—for everybody is "goin' feast off'n milk an' honey.

2. Black slaves also expressed their anticipation of God's new future with apocalyptic imagination. "Where shall I be when the first trumpet soun'; soun' so loud till it woke up de dead?" "One day, one day 'bout twelve o'clock, O this ol' earth goin' reel an' rock." "O My Lord, what a morning, when the stars begin to fall!" "When the sun refuse to shine, when the moon goes down in blood!" "In dat great getting up morning," "de world will be on fire," and "you'll see de stars a-fallin', de forked lightning, de coffins bursting," and "de righteous marching." "The dumb will talk, the lame will walk, the blind will see, and the deaf will hear."

These songs emphasized the inability of the present to contain the reality of the divine future. In this sense the spirituals were "otherworldly." They stressed the utter distinction between the present and the future. The hope of black slaves was not of this world, not in the "hell of a completely understood humanity." [10] They hoped for "the One who is never knowable, who, in the constant revolution and 'transformation' within faith, is alone disclosed as a promise."[11] It was a hope *against* the hopes of this world, against the self-erected gods of finite people. It was hope *for* the God of the Exodus, of the prophets, and of the resurrected Christ, whose will is known through the promise disclosed in his liberating activity in history. And it is through the strength of their hope in God that the oppressed are saved (Romans 8:24).

It was this transcendent element of hope (as expressed in black music) which elevated black people above the limitations of the slave experience, and enabled them to view black humanity independently of their oppressors. Through music black slaves ritualized their existence and gave to their lives a dimension of promise and new reality that could not be contained in human theologies and philosophies. As they accepted the promise and took it to themselves, it became a real force in their history; hence "a new dimension of promise and new reality." The concept of heaven in black music placed the people in a "New Earth" and transformed their perceptions of black existence from the nothingness of the present condition of slavery into being-for-the-future. Heaven was a vision of a new Black Humanity.

Some critics will observe that even if black eschatology is interpreted as something other than a description of the geography of the next world, it still introduces a jarringly non-historical element into the analysis of liberation. It speaks of an ultimate liberation that is primarily of God and not of human beings, of the next world and not this world. If authentic liberation is a *historical* reality (having to do with economics, politics, and the sociality of human existence), how can it be reconciled with "A-settin' down with Jesus, Eatin' honey and drinkin' wine, Marchin' round de throne, Wid Peter, James, and John"? What possible relationship could the "gospel feast" have with the politics of Black Power, or the Marxist's claim that liberation is a historical determination of which the human being is sole agent? As Gajo Petrovic, interpreting Marx, put it: *"The question of the essence of freedom,* like the question of the essence of man, *is not only a question.* It is *at once participation in production of freedom.* It is an activity through which freedom frees itself."[12] Is not heaven an opium, a clever religious trick devised by oppressors so that the oppressed will not challenge their rule on earth? True, white oppressors did preach "pie in the sky" as a means to get black people to accept their exploitation. But white oppressors have also used, over the years, distorted versions of Democracy, Marxism, and even Black Power as their means to confuse and control the oppressed, and they will distort any world-view to camouflage their own interests.

Accordingly, the problems of black religion today will not be solved by rejecting it outright, simply because white people have misused black religion for their own selfish interests. The task, however, of black theologians is to move beyond the distortions of black religion to the authentic substance of black religious experience so that it can continue to serve as a positive force in liberating black people. And black theologians will find that the strongest counterweight to the obstacles in the way of historical liberation is that vision of the future defined by the oppressed black slaves. As Walter Benjamin has observed: "It is only for the sake of those without hope that hope is given for us."[13]

Behind the apocalyptic vision of powerless black slaves there was precisely this openness to the future which moved them beyond their finite capabilities. From the midst of their very enslavement they looked *forward* to the time of deliverance when they would leave the unbearable oppression of the world around them. To them this looking forward was no mere role assigned to them in an apocalyptic myth; it was an authentic account of what they were experiencing and struggling with as slaves. Black slaves believed that when people become submissive because they are afraid of the future, God remains the absolute future and continues the divine work of liberation even though people are passive and inactive. When the people of Israel complained to Moses about the approaching Egyptian army, preferring the fleshpots of Egypt to the uncertainty of the future, God said: "Tell the people of Israel to go *forward*" (Exodus 14:15). Authentic human liberation is found only in the struggle for the future that is grounded in divine liberation. The "divine element" stands for that reality in human encounter which will not let people remain content with slavery, injustice, and oppression.

Judgment and the Righteousness of God

What is actually at stake in the image of heaven is the righteousness of God. The central theme of biblical religion is the justice of God. Yahweh is known by what God does in history, and what God does is always identical with the liberation of the poor from the injustice of the strong.

> For he delivers the needy when he calls,
>   the poor and him who has no helper.
> He has pity on the weak and the needy,
>   and saves the lives of the needy.
> From oppression and violence he redeems their life;
>   and precious is their blood in his sight.
>   Ps. 72:12-14

The righteousness of God is the power of God to achieve victory for the oppressed. If this biblical message is true, how then does God redeem the already dead slaves who did not have an opportunity to achieve true humanity? What does God's righteousness mean for black people who have died because they were powerless to defend themselves against white overlords? The black slaves' answer to this problem of theodicy was found in their image of heaven. They affirmed that Christ's resurrection from the dead is the divine guarantee that they have a future that cannot be destroyed by death. On the cross God took their place and transformed the contradictions of the present into an openness of the future. The event of the resurrection is the disclosure of the power of God's righteousness unto salvation, God's will to make plain that there is a future for the weak which is not made with human hands. Heaven, in the black spirituals, was an affirmation of this hope in the absolute power of God's righteousness as revealed in God's future.

In the Old Testament, the judgment of God was inseparable from divine righteousness. God's judgment was the unveiling of God's righteousness in history. It was God delivering the poor and needy from the injustice of the rich and strong. In this sense, the judgment of God was already happening wherever the oppressed were being liberated. This was what one ex-slave had in mind when she said: "God is punishing some of them old suckers and their children right now for the way they use to treat us poor colored folks."[14]

The idea of judgment was related also to the *end* of time. According to the New Testament, "Christ himself will come to judge both the living and the dead, and all men will stand before his judgment seat" (Matt. 25:31f., Acts 17:31, II Cor. 5:10).[15] The emphasis was on the full revelation of God's righteousness that will come at the *end* of history and which will be inaugurated by the Second Coming of Jesus Christ. Interpreting the biblical concept of judgment, N. H. Snaith said:

Nothing less than the end of history is involved, and with it a visible manifestation of Christ on this earth, and a demonstration of his eternal victory in the salvation of those who have faith in him and the destruction of those who persist in rebellion.[16]

Black slaves accepted the biblical concept of judgment. For them judgment will be the time when Christ comes to judge the living and the dead. The righteous will be received into the heavenly

kingdom amid rejoicing and shouting. The wicked will be punished in hell.

> Then they'll cry out for cold water
> While the Christians shout in glory
> Saying Amen to their damnation
> Fare you well, fare you well.

Judgment was understood as an inevitable element in God's
fulfillment of the divine promise. No one will be able to avoid
it because "My Lord says He's gwineter rain down fire."

> Dere's no hidin' place down dere,
> Dere's no hidin' place down dere,
> Oh I went to de rock to hide my face,
> De rock cried out, "No hidin' place,"
> Dere's no hidin' place down dere.

> Oh de rock cried, "I'm burnin' too,"
> Oh de rock cried, "I'm burnin' too,"
> Oh de rock cried, "I'm burnin' too,
> I want a go to hebbin as well as you,"
> Dere's no hidin' place down dere.

Judgment was the time when everyone would have to give an
account of his or her earthly behavior.

> Got to go to judgment stand your trial,
> Got to go to judgment stand your trial,
> Got to go to judgment stand your trial,
> Can't stay away.

It was a time of reaping the consequences of ethical actions.

> You shall reap jes what you sow,
> You shall reap jes what you sow,
> On the mountain, in the valley,
> You shall reap jes what you sow.

Because black slaves believed that they had been faithful to God's righteousness, they did not fear God's coming judgment. Indeed, they welcomed its coming.

> Blow your trumpet, Gabriel, Blow louder, louder;
> And I hope dat trumpet might blow me home to de
> new Jerusalem.

They welcomed God's judgment because it would uncover their new, true personhood.

> O, nobody knows who I am,
> Till the judgment morning.

Black identity is bound up with God's future judgment, and at the moment of this awareness black liberation becomes a full reality.

With reference to black eschatology, four concluding assertions can be made. (1) Black eschatology was based on historical possibilities. According to the black spirituals, belief in God's future meant accepting the burden and the risk of escape to the North and later Canada. (2) When black slaves realized that their historical possibilities were limited, they began to create structures of black affirmation which protected their humanity even though they could not escape the chains of slavery. (3) Black eschatology also meant an affirmation of life after death. The concept of heaven meant that God's righteousness, as revealed in the liberation of the oppressed, was sovereign. God alone was the ultimate Lord of history. The wicked will be punished and the victim will be vindicated. (4) The most crucial ingredient of black eschatology was its *historicity*. Even when it was no longer feasible to expect radical historical evidence of God's liberation of the oppressed, black slaves' image of God's future righteousness was always related to their present existence on earth. Eschatology then was primarily a religious perspective on the present which enabled oppressed blacks to realize that their existence transcended historical limitations. This emphasis is, perhaps, the most important contribution of black religion as reflected in the spirituals.

In view of the emphasis of black eschatology on the certainty of divine liberation of the oppressed from earthly bondage, I contend that it provides the best theological foundation for a truly radical interpretation of the future. Recently there has been much discussion among American and European theologians about humanizing the world according to God's promised future. But the future about which they speak is too abstract and too unrelated to the history and culture of black people who have been and are being dehumanized and dehistoricized by white imperialists and colonialists. As a black theologian, I believe that authentic Christian hope must be defined by the oppressed's vision of the expectant future and not by philosophical abstractions. Christian hope is a vision and a promise for the poor, the sick, and the weak; and they hope for a new heaven and a new earth. Their hope is *against* the present order of injustice and slavery and *for* a new order of justice and peace. And unless theology takes seriously the hope of the suffering for historical liberation, it will remain irrelevant for the oppressed who view the gospel as the good news of freedom.

With all the recent talk among American theologians about "hope theology," "humanistic messianism," "Marxist-Christian dialogue," and revolutionary theology, one would expect that such language could easily be related to black people and their thoughts on the future and divine liberation. But that is not true. White American theologians have been virtually silent on black liberation, preferring instead to do theology in the light of a modern liberalism that assumes that black people want to integrate into the white way of life. Such silence is inexcusable, and it is hard not to conclude that those who maintain it are enslaved by their own identity with the culture and history of the slave masters. What these theologians themselves need is liberation, and that will only happen when they face the reality of Black Power and what that means for the oppressed of the land.

One of the effective starting points for this much-needed grappling with reality are the black spirituals which came to maturity in the ante-bellum years, and which expressed the profound hope of God's enslaved people in God's liberated future.

6

The Blues:
A Secular Spiritual

What did I do
To be so black
And blue?

Theologically, there is more to be said about the music of black
people than what was revealed in the black spirituals. To be
sure, a significant number of black people were confident that
the God of Israel was involved in black history, liberating them
from slavery and oppression. But not all blacks could accept the
divine promises of the Bible as a satisfactory answer to the contradictions of black existence. They refused to adopt a God-
centered perspective as the solution to the problem of black
suffering. Instead, they sang, "Got the blues, and too dam' mean
to cry."

The blues depict the "secular" dimension of black experience. They are "worldly" songs which tell us about love and sex
and about that other "mule kickin' in my stall." They tell us
about the "Black Cat's Bones," "a Mojo hand," and "dese back-
bitin' womens tryin' fo' to steal my man." The blues are about
black life and the sheer earth and gut capacity to survive in an
extreme situation of oppression.

> I wrote these blues, gonna sing 'em as I please,
> I wrote these blues, gonna sing 'em as I please,

I'm the only one like the way I'm singin' 'em,
I'll swear to goodness ain't no one else to please.

The Rise of the Blues

The exact date of the origin of the blues is difficult to determine. Most experts agree that they probably began to take form in the late nineteenth century.[1] But the spirit and mood of the blues have roots stretching back into slavery days and even to Africa. As with the spirituals, the Africanism of the blues is related to the *functional* character of West African music. And this is one of the essential ingredients of black music which distinguishes it from Western music and connects it with its African heritage. "The fact that American Negro music, like the African, is at the core of daily life explains the immemorial African quality of all Negro *folk* music in this country, if not of the Negro in exile everywhere."[2]

Black music, then, is not an artistic creation for its own sake; rather it tells us about the *feeling* and *thinking* of an African people, and the kinds of mental adjustments they had to make in order to survive in an alien land. For example, the work songs were a means of heightening energy, converting labor into dances and games, and providing emotional excitement in an otherwise unbearable situation. The emphasis was on free, continuous, creative energy as produced in song.[3] A similar functional character applied to the slave seculars, ballads, spirituals, as well as the blues.

Slavery is the historical background out of which the blues were created. From a theological perspective, the blues are closely related to the "slave seculars." The "secular" songs of slavery were "non-religious," occasionally anti-religious, and were often called "devil songs" by religious folk. The "seculars" expressed the skepticism of black slaves who found it difficult to take seriously anything suggesting the religious faith of white preachers. Sterling Brown reported:

Bible stories, especially the creation, the fall of Man, and the flood, were spoofed. "Reign, Master Jesus, reign" became "Rain Masser, rain hard! Rain flour and lard, and a big hog head, Down in my back yard." After couplets of nonsense and ribaldry, slaves sang with their fingers crossed, or hopeless in defeat: "Po' mourner, you shall be free, when de good Lord set you free."[4]

While seculars were not strictly atheistic as defined by modern Western philosophy, they nonetheless uncover the difficulties black people encountered when they attempted to relate white Christian categories to their situation of oppression.

The blues reflect the same existential tension. Taking form sometime after the Emancipation and Reconstruction, they invited black people to embrace the reality and truth of black experience. They express the "laments of folk Negroes over hard luck, 'careless' or unrequited love, broken family life, or general dissatisfaction with a cold and trouble-filled world."[5] And implied in the blues is a stubborn refusal to go beyond the existential problem and substitute otherworldly answers. It is not that the blues reject God; rather, they *ignore* God by embracing the joys and sorrows of life, such as those of a man's relationship with his woman, a woman with her man.

> Ef you don't want me, baby, ain't got to carry no stall.
> I can get mo' women than a passenger train can haul.
>
> Gonna build me a scaffold, I'm gonna hang myself.
> Cain't get the man I love, don't want no body else.

Because the blues ignore the "religious" concerns of the church, many interpreters of black music make a sharp distinction between the blues and the spirituals. John W. Work's treatment is representative:

> The blues differ radically from the spirituals. . . . The spirituals are intensely religious, and the blues are just as intensely worldly. The spirituals sing of heaven, and of the fervent hope that after death the singer may enjoy the celestial joys to be found there. The blues singer has no interest in heaven, and not much hope in earth—a thor-

oughly disillusioned individual. The spirituals were created in the church; the blues sprang from everyday life.[6]

Unfortunately, it is true that many black church people at first condemned the blues as vulgar and indecent. But that was because they did not understand them rightly. If the blues are viewed in the proper perspective, it is clear that their mood is very similar to the ethos of the spirituals. Indeed, I contend that the blues and the spirituals flow from the same bedrock of experience, and neither is an adequate interpretation of black life without the commentary of the other. "The blues issued directly out of . . . the spiritual."[7] They express and formalize a mood already present in the spirituals. For example, the spirituals, *Nobody knows the trouble I've seen; I'm rollin' through an unfriendly world; I'm a-trouble in the mind; Sometimes I feel like a motherless child; Sometimes I hangs my head and cries* anticipated the "worried blues." That was why Leadbelly (Huddie Ledbetter) said: "Blues was composed up by the Negro people when they was under slavery. They was worried."[8]

The blues are "secular spirituals."[9] They are *secular* in the sense that they confine their attention solely to the immediate and affirm the bodily expression of black soul, including its sexual manifestations. They are *spirituals* because they are impelled by the same search for the truth of black experience.

Yet despite the fact that the blues and the spirituals partake of the same black experience, there are important differences between them. The spirituals are *slave* songs, and they deal with historical realities that are pre-Civil War. They were created and sung by the group. The blues, while having some pre-Civil War roots, are essentially post-Civil War in consciousness. They reflect experiences that issued from Emancipation, the Reconstruction Period, and segregation laws. "The blues was conceived," writes LeRoi Jones, "by freedmen and ex-slaves—if not as a result of a personal or intellectual experience, at least as an emotional confirmation of, and reaction to, the way in which most Negroes were still forced to exist in the United States."[10] Also, in contrast to the group singing of the spirituals, the blues are intensely personal and individualistic.

Historically and theologically, the blues express conditions

associated with the "burden of freedom." However, freedom in
the blues is not simply the "existential freedom" defined by
modern philosophy. Philosophical existentialism speaks of freedom in the context of absurdity and about the inability to reconcile the "strangeness of the world" with one's perception of
human existence. But absurdity in the blues is factual, not con-
ceptual. The blues, while not denying that the world was strange,
described its strangeness in more concrete and vivid terms. Freedom took on historical specificity when contrasted with legal
servitude. It meant that simple alternatives, which whites took
for granted, became momentous options for newly "free" black
slaves. It meant getting married, drinking gin, praising God—
and expressing these historical possibilities in song.

The Emancipation decentralized the black population, and
the Reconstruction gave black people a certain feeling of auton-
omy and self-reliance that they had not experienced during slavery. For the first time, many black people were free to move
from town to town and from farm to farm, without being
restricted by slave codes and patrollers. They had leisure and
the freedom to be alone and to reflect. But these options also
revealed new limitations. To be sure, blacks had free time, but
they also needed money for food and shelter.

> I never had to have no money befo',
> And now they want it everywhere I go.

The Hayes Compromise of 1877 led to the withdrawal of
federal troops from the South and ended the hopes of black
people becoming authentic participants in the political processes
of America. In 1883 the United States Supreme Court declared
the Civil Rights Act of 1875 as unconstitutional; and in 1896 it
upheld the doctrine of "separate but equal" (Plessy vs. Fergu-
son), giving legal sanction to the dehumanizing aspects of white
supremacy. By the end of the nineteenth century, the political
disfranchisement of black people was complete. White people
could still do to black people what they willed, just as in slavery
days. This was the situation that created the blues. As LeRoi
Jones puts it:

The Negro could not ever become white and that was his
strength; at some point, always, he could not participate
in the dominant tenor of the white man's culture. It was
at this juncture that he had to make use of other resources,
whether African, sub-cultural, or hermetic. And it was this
boundary, this no man's land, that provided the logic and
beauty of his music.[11]

During slavery the social movement of black people was limited, and the church served as the primary social unit for black
expression. After the Civil War, the social mobility of blacks
increased, and the church became only one of several places
where blacks could meet and talk about the problems of black
existence. Other "priests" of the community began to emerge
alongside of the preachers and deacons; and other songs were
sung in addition to the spirituals. The "new priests" of the black
community were the blues men and women; and their songs
were the blues. Like the preacher in the church, they proclaimed
the Word of black existence, depicting its joy and sorrow, love
and hate, and the awesome burden of being "free" in a racist
society when one is black.

> Oh, Ahm tired a dis mess,
> Oh, yes, Ahm tired a dis mess.

Toward a Definition of the Blues

What is the precise meaning of the blues? And how is that
meaning related to the experience of the black community?
These questions are not easy to answer, because the blues do
not deal with abstract ideas that can be analyzed from the perspective of "objective reason." They are not propositional truths
about the black experience. Rather they are the essential ingredients that define the *essence* of the black experience. And to
understand them, it is necessary to view the blues as a *state of
mind in relation to the Truth of the black experience.* This is what
blues man Henry Townsend, of St. Louis, has in mind when he
says: "When I sing the blues I sing the truth."[12]
The blues and Truth are one reality of the black experience.

The blues are that "true feeling," says Henry Townsend.[13] Or as Furry Lewis of Memphis puts it: "All the blues, you can say, is true."[14] The blues are true because they combine art and life, poetry and experience, the symbolic and the real. They are an artistic response to the chaos of life. And to sing the blues truthfully, it is necessary to experience the historical realities that created them. In the words of Memphis Willie B.: "A blues is about something that's real. It is about what a man feels when his wife leaves him, or about some disappointment that happens to him that he can't do anything about. That's why none of these young boys can really sing the blues. They don't know about the things that go into a blues."[15]

The thing that goes into the blues is the experience of being black in a white racist society. It is that peculiar feeling that makes you know that there is something seriously wrong with the society, even though you may not possess the intellectual or political power to do anything about it. No black person can escape the blues, because the blues are an inherent part of black existence in America. To be black is to be blue. Leadbelly is right: "All Negroes like the blues . . . because they was born with the blues."[16] This truth is expressed in the lyrics:

> If de blues was whiskey,
> I'd stay drunk all de time.
>
> If de blues was money,
> I'd be a millioneer.

For many people, a blues song is about sex or a lonely woman longing for her rambling man. However, the blues are more than that. To be sure, the blues involve sex and what that means for human bodily expression, but on a much deeper level.

> De blues ain't nothin'
> But a poor man's heart disease.

The blues express a black perspective on the incongruity of life and the attempt to achieve meaning in a situation fraught with contradictions. As Aunt Molly Jackson of Kentucky put it:

"The blues are made by working people. ... when they have a
lot of problems to solve about their work, when their wages are
low and they don't have no way to exist hardly and they don't
know which way to turn and what to do."[17] Blind Lemon Jefferson expresses a similar feeling in song:

> I stood on the corner, and I almost bust my head,
> I stood on the corner, almost bust my head,
> I couldn't earn me enough money to buy me a loaf
>   of bread.

The blues experience always is an encounter with life, its
trials and tribulations, its bruises and abuses—but not without
benefit of the melody and rhythm of song.

> When a woman takes de blues,
> She tucks her head and cries.
> But when a man catches the blues,
> He catches er freight and rides.

Through song a new dimension is created and the individual is
transported to another level of experience. Blues music is music
of the black soul, the music of the black psyche renewing itself
for living and being.

> People, I've stood these blues 'bout as long as I can.
> I walked all night with these blues, we both joined
>   hand in hand.
> And they travelled my heart through, just like a
>   natural man.

The blues are an expression of fortitude in the face of a
broken existence. They emphasize the will to be, despite nonbeing as symbolized in racism and hate.

> Lord, going to sleep now for mama just got bad news,
> Lord, going to sleep now for mama just got bad news,
> To try to dream away my troubles, counting the blues.

The blues are a state of mind that affirms the essential worth of black humanity, even though white people attempted to define blacks as animals. The blues tell us about a people who refused to accept the absurdity of white society. Black people rebelled artistically, and affirmed through ritual, pattern, and form that they were human beings. "You never seen a mule sing, have you?" asked Big Bill (William Lee Conley) Broonzy.

The affirmation of self in the blues is the emphasis that connects them theologically with the spirituals. Like the spirituals, the blues affirm the somebodiness of black people, and they preserve the worth of black humanity through ritual and drama. The blues are a transformation of black life through the sheer power of song. They symbolize the solidarity, the attitudes, and the identity of the black community and thus create the emotional forms of reference for endurance and esthetic appreciation. In this sense, the blues are that stoic feeling that recognizes the painfulness of the present but refuses to surrender to its historical contradictions.

The blues tell us how black people affirmed their existence and refused to be destroyed by the oppressive environment; how, despite white definitions to the contrary, they defined their own somebodiness and realized that America was not their true home.

> Ain't it hard to stumble,
> When you got no place to fall?
> In this whole wide world,
> I ain't got no place at all.

The blues feeling was not just a temporary "bad mood" that would soon pass away. The blues have to do with the structure and meaning of existence itself. Black people were asking questions about the nature of being and non-being, life and death. They knew that something was wrong; people were not created to be defined by others. And neither was it meant for a woman to be separated from her man. And Clara Smith pleads for a prescription for "de mean ole blues."

> All day long I'm worried;
> All day long I'm blue;

I'm so awfully lonesome,
I doan know what to do.

So I ask yo', Doctor,
See if you can fin'
Somethin' in yo' satchel
To pacify my min'.

Doctor! Doctor!
Write me a prescription fo' dih blues.
De mean ole blues.

Because the blues are rooted in the black perception of existence, they are historical. They focus on concrete events of everyday existence. When asked about the origin of the blues, Son House of Mississippi replied:

All I can say is that when I was a boy we always was singin' in the fields. Not real singin', you know, just hollerin'. But we made up our songs about things that was happenin' to us at the time, and I think that's where the blues started.[18]

Historical experience, as interpreted by the black community, is the key to an understanding of the blues. Black people accepted the dictum: Truth is experience, and experience is the Truth. If it is lived and encountered, then it is real. There is no attempt in the blues to make philosophical distinctions between divine and human truth. That is why many blues people reject the contention that the blues are vulgar or dirty. As Henry Townsend puts it: "If I sing the blues and tell the truth, what have I done? What have I committed? I haven't lied."[19]

The blues tell us about the strength of black people to survive, to endure, and to shape existence while living in the midst of oppressive contradictions. They also tell us about the joy and sweetness of love.

Hey mama! Hey girl!
Don't you hear me calling you?

You're so sweet, so sweet,
My baby, so sweet.

Say I love you baby, love her to the bone.
I hate to see my sweet sugar go home.
She's so sweet, so sweet,
My little woman, so sweet.

See my baby coming, don't get so smart.
I'll cut you just a little above your heart.
She's so sweet, so sweet,
My little woman, so sweet.

The blues also deal with the agony of love. The blues woman is the priestess and prophet of the people. She verbalizes the emotion for herself and the audience, articulating the stresses and strains of human relationships.

My man left this morning, just about half past four.
My man left this morning, just about half past four.
He left a note on the pillow saying he couldn't use
     me no more.

I grabbed my pillow, turned over in my bed.
I grabbed my pillow, turned over in my bed.
I cried about my daddy until my cheeks turned cherry
     red.

It's awful hard to take it, it was such a bitter pill.
It's awful hard to take it, it was such a bitter pill.
If the blues don't kill me that man's meanness will.

The blues are not abstract; they are concrete. They are intense and direct responses to the reality of black experience. They tell us about floods, pneumonia, and the train. The train was a symbol of escape from the harsh reality of the present. It was the freedom to move and many blacks "got on board," expressing their liberated being.

> Some day ah'm gonna lay down dis heavy load,
> Gonna grab me a train,
> Gonna clam aboh'd.
>
> Gonna go up No'th,
> Gonna ease mah pain,
> Yessuh, Lord, gonna catch dat train.

Every aspect of black life was exemplified in the blues. There are blues about prisons, highways, and the St. Louis storm.

> The shack where we was livin', she reeled and rock
>   but never fell—Lord have mercy!
> The shack where we was livin', she reeled and rock
>   but never fell—Lord have mercy!
> How that cyclone started, nobody but the Lord can
>   tell.

The blues dealt with TB and other forms of sickness. They focused on guns, highways, the Greyhound buses, and the boll weevil. The boll weevil was that little black bug that invaded Texas over fifty years ago, and destroyed more than a billion dollars in cotton. It was nearly indestructible. Though black people were the chief victims, they also admired it for its power of endurance. Like Brer Rabbit in black folklore, the weevil was the symbol of the small defeating the rich and mighty.

> The Boll Weevil is a little black bug
> Come from Mexico, they say,
> He come to try the Texas soil,
> Just lookin' for a place to stay;
>   Just lookin' for a home,
>   Just lookin' for a home.
>
> The farmer took the Boll Weevil
> And put him in the hot sand;
> The Weevil say "This is mighty hot,
> But I'll stand it like a man

For it is my home,
This'll be my home."

Boll Weevil say to the doctor,
"You can throw out all your pills;
When I get through with the farmer,
He won't pay no doctor bills:
    Won't have no home,
    He won't have no home."

Merchant got half the cotton,
Boll Weevil got the rest;
Didn't leave the poor farmer's wife
But one old cotton dress,
    And it's full of holes,
    Yes, it's full of holes.

The blues were living reality. They are a sad feeling and also
a joyous mood. They are bitter but also sweet. They are funny
and not so funny. The blues are not evil per se; rather they
represent that sad feeling when a woman's man leaves or joy
when he returns. They are part of that structure of reality in
which human beings are condemned to live. And because the
black person had to live in the midst of a broken existence, the
reality of the blues was stark and real.

Well, the blues ain't nothin'
But a workingman feelin' bad.
Well, it's one of the worst old feelin's
That any poor man's ever had.

The personification of the blues feeling and experience is
most revealing: to black folk he is no shadow, but a person whose
presence is inescapable.

I worry all day, I worry all night,
Everytime my man comes home he wants to fuss and
    fight.

> When I pick up the paper to try to read the news,
> Just when I'm satisfied, yonder comes the blues.

This blues person is no stranger, but somebody every black knows well. For "When I got up this mornin', [the] Blues [was] walking round my bed; I went to eat my breakfast, the blues was in my bread." And I said:

> Good mornin', blues,
> Blues, how do you do?
> Yes, blues, how do you do?
> I'm doing all right,
> Good mornin', how are you?

The Blues and Black Suffering

The origin and definition of the blues cannot be understood independent of the suffering that black people endured in the context of white racism and hate. Therefore, the question that gave shape and purpose to the blues was: How could black people keep themselves together, preserving a measure of their cultural being, and not lose their physical lives? Responding to the significance of that question for the black community, blues people sang:

> Times is so tough, can't even get a dime,
> Yes times is so tough, can't even get a dime,
> Times don't get better, I'm going to lose my mind.

The blues tell us about black people's attempt to carve out a significant existence in a very trying situation. The purpose of the blues is to give structure to black existence in a context where color means rejection and humiliation.

Suffering and its relation to blackness is inseparable from the meaning of the blues. Without pain and suffering, and what that meant for black people in Mississippi, Tennessee, and Arkansas, there would have been no blues. The blue mood means sorrow, frustration, despair, and black people's attempt to take these existential realities upon themselves and not lose their sanity.

The blues are not art for art's sake, music for music's sake. They are a way of life, a life-style of the black community; and they came into being to give expression to black identity and the will for survival. Thus to seek to understand the blues apart from the suffering that created them is to misinterpret them and distort the very creativity that defines them. This is what Clarence Williams, a New York publisher who has written many blues, meant when he said:

> Why, I'd never have written blues if I had been white. You don't study to write the blues, you *feel* them. It's the mood you're in—sometimes it's a rainy day . . . just like the time I lay for hours in a swamp in Louisiana. Spanish moss dripping everywhere . . . White men were looking for me with guns—I wasn't scared, just sorry I didn't have a gun. I began to hum a tune—a little sighing kinda tune—you know like this. . . . "Jes as blue as a tree—an old willow tree—nobody 'round here, jes nobody but me."[20]

It is impossible to sing the blues or listen to their authentic presentation without recognizing that they belong to a particular community. They were created in the midst of the black struggle for being. And because the blues are an expression of that struggle, they are inseparable from blackness and trouble. That is why Henry Townsend says that the distinctive quality of the good blues singer is "Trouble . . . that's right. That's the one word solution. Trouble. You know you can only express a true feeling if you're sincere about it. You can only express what happened to you."[21]

The trouble that makes the blues is not just the particular difficulties of an individual blues singer. It involves much more than that. The trouble of the blues refers to the history of a people, and the kinds of difficulties they encountered in their struggle for existence. As John Lee Hooker puts it:

> When I sing the blues . . . it's not . . . that I had the hardships that a lot of people had throughout the South and other cities throughout the country, but I do know what they went through . . . it's not only what happened to you—

it's what happened to your foreparents and other people.
And that's what makes the blues.[22]

The blues, as Charley Patton sang about them, are a *"Mean
Black Moan."* They recognize that there is something wrong with
this world, something absurd about the way that white people
treat black people. The blues singer articulates this mood, and
thus provides a degree of transcendence over the troubles of
this world. When the blues caught the absurdity of black existence in white America and vividly and artistically expressed it
in word and suitable music, it afforded black people a certain
distance from their immediate trouble and allowed them to see
and feel it artistically, thereby offering them a certain liberating
catharsis. That black people could transcend trouble without
ignoring it means that they were not destroyed by it.

But the questions can be asked: How could black people
endure the stresses and strains of segregation and lynchings and
not lose their sanity? If the blues were, as LeRoi Jones said, the
result of thought,[23] what do they tell us about black people's
reflections on their pain and sorrow? What is the explanation
of black suffering in the blues? It is important to observe that
the blues, like the spirituals, were not written or sung for the
purpose of answering the "problem of evil." They merely
describe the reality of black suffering without seeking to devise
philosophical solutions for the problem of absurdity. In this
sense, the blues are *existential*; that is, they assume that reality
inherent in historical existence and not in abstract essence. That
is why there is much emphasis on the concrete restrictions
placed on the black community, and why color is a dominant
theme of the blues.

> Now, if you're white
>   You're all right,
> If you're brown,
>   Stick aroun'
> But if you're black
>   Git back! Git back! Git back!

The blues do not speak about abstract humanity but about
particular men and women who encounter the trials and tribu-

lations of human existence. They tell us about that "po' boy long way from home" and about "de freight train . . . sixteen coaches long." The blues are about "goin' up North, where they say money grows on trees," but "I don't give a doggone, if my black soul leaves." They are about love and sex and the pain of human relationships. They are also about death.

> You know I got my suitcase and took on down the
>   road,
> Uumh, took on down the road,
> But when I got there, she was laying on the cooling
>   bo'd.

The response to suffering in the blues is, however, different from what we saw earlier in the spirituals. According to the spirituals, blacks of slavery could endure oppression because they believed that the God of Israel would eventually set them free. The spirituals do not reflect the problem of theodicy since black people did not identify God as being responsible for their slavery. Instead, their concern was for God not to leave them alone in a world full of trouble. The blues people, however, sing as if God is irrelevant, and their task is to deal with trouble without special reference to Jesus Christ. This is not atheism; rather, it is believing that *transcendence* will only be meaningful when it is made real in and through the limits of historical experience. The achievement of being is an entirely historical reality, grounded and defined within the context of the community's experience. The blues people believe that it is only through the acceptance of the real as disclosed in concrete human affairs that a community can attain authentic existence.

While the blues reject an "objective transcendence," they do not reject "historical transcendence." Insofar as the blues affirm the somebodiness of black people, they are transcendent reflections on black humanity. Through the sheer power of melody and rhythm of song, black people transcended historical restrictions and affirmed a meaning for their lives not made with hands. They refused to accept white rules and regulations as the definition of their community. To be sure, they cried, "I got the blues an' can't keep from cryin'." They were hurt, and they were bruised. But through the sharing of their troubles with each other, black people were able to move to another level of human existence and be, in spite of the non-being of the white community. That is why they could sing:

> I got the world in a jug,
> The stopper in my hand.

The important contribution of the blues is their affirmation of black humanity in the face of immediate absurdity. Although blacks were beaten and shot, they refused to allow their perception of black humanity to be reduced to the sum total of their brutalization. They transcended the restrictions of history by affirming that perception of black humanity revealed in and through the historical struggle for being.

The Blues and Sex

Because we know that we have survived, that we have not been destroyed, and that we are more than the stripes on our backs, we can sing as a way of celebrating our being. Indeed, for black people, existence is a form of celebration. It is joy, love, and sex. It is hugging, kissing, and feeling. People cannot love physically and spiritually (the two cannot be separated!) until they have been up against the edge of life, experiencing the hurt and pain of existence. They cannot appreciate the feel and touch of life nor express the beauty of giving themselves to each other in community, in love, and in sex until they know and experience the brokenness of existence as disclosed in human oppression. People who have not been oppressed physically cannot know the power inherent in bodily expressions of love. That is why white Western culture makes a sharp distinction between the spirit and the body, the divine and the human, the sacred and the secular. White oppressors do not know how to come to terms with the essential *spiritual* function of the human body. But for black people the body is sacred, and they know how to use it in the expression of love.

Most interpreters agree that the dominant and most expressive theme in the blues is sex. Whatever else is said about them,

the blues cannot be understood if this important theme is omit-
ted. As blues man Furry Lewis puts it: "The blues come from a
woman wanting to see her man, and a man wanting to see his
woman." Or, as Henry Townsend says: "You know, that's the
major thing in life. Please believe me. What you love the best is
what can hurt you the most." Ma Rainey also puts it well:

> People have different blues and think they're mighty
>   sad,
> But blues about a man the worst I ever had . . .

And another says:

> You know my woman left me,
> Left me cold in hand.
> I wouldn't hate it so bad,
> But she left with another man.

The blues are the songs of men and women who have been hurt
and disappointed and who feel the confusion and isolation of
human love.

> 'Gwine lay my head right on de railroad track,
> 'Gwine lay my head right on de railroad track,
> Cause my baby, she won't take me back.

The blue mood is about black men and women — their lament,
grief, and disillusionment. In a world where a people possess
little that is their own, human relationships are placed at a high
premium. The love between men and women becomes immediate and real. Black people live in that kind of world; and they
express the pain of separation and loneliness.

> Did you ever wake up in the morning, find your man
>   had gone?
> Did you ever wake up in the morning, find your man
>   had gone?
> You will wring your hands, you will cry the whole day
>   long.

But the blues were not just sad feelings about separation, the loss of a man or woman. There was also humor about sexuality.

> Good lookin' woman make a bull dog break his chain,
> Good lookin' woman make a bull dog break his chain,
> Good lookin' woman make a snail catch a passenger
>   train.

> Yaller gal make a preacher lay his Bible down,
> Yaller gal make a preacher lay his Bible down,
> Good lookin' high brown make him run from town
>   to town.

> Good lookin' woman make a mule kick his stable
>   down,
> Good lookin' woman make a mule kick his stable
>   down,
> Good lookin' woman make a rabbit move his family
>   to town.

> Woman without a man like a ship without a sail,
> Woman without a man like a ship without a sail,
> Ship without a sail like a dog without a tail.

There is seriousness, too, when a man appeals to his woman to make up her mind.

> If you didn't want me girlie what made you say you
>   do,
> If you didn't want me girlie what made you say you
>   do,
> Take your time little girl, nobody's rushin' you.

The blues are honest music. They describe every aspect of a woman's feelings about a man, and what a man thinks about a woman. Through the blues, black people express their views about infidelity and sex. The blues woman said:

> You can cheat on me, you can steal on me,
>   you can fool me all along.

You can cheat on me, you can steal on me,
    you can fool me all along.
All I ask you daddy, please don't let me catch you
    wrong.

And her man answered:

I'm a hard-working man and, baby, I don't mind
    dying,
I'm a hard-working man and, baby, I don't mind
    dying,
I catch you cheating on me, then, baby, you don't
    mind dying.

It has been the vivid description of sex that caused many church people to reject the blues as vulgar or dirty. The Christian tradition has always been ambiguous about sexual intercourse, holding it to be divinely ordained yet the paradigm of rebellious passion. Perhaps this accounts for the absence of sex in the black spirituals and other black church music. But most blacks only verbalized the distinction between the "sacred" and "profane" and found themselves unable to follow white Christianity's rejection of the body. And those who did not experience the free acceptance of sexual love on Saturday nights, expressed it indirectly on Sunday mornings through song and sermon.

In the blues there is an open acceptance of sexual love, and it is described in most vivid terms: "She moves it just right," "I'm going to have it now," "It hurts me so good," "Do it a long time," "Warm it up to me," "Drive it down," "Slow driving."

Peach Orchard Mama, you swore nobod'd pick your
    fruit but me,
Peach Orchard Mama, you swore nobod'd pick your
    fruit but me,
I found three kid men shaking down your peaches
    free.

What are we to make of such blatant descriptions of sexual love? Theologically, the blues reject the Greek distinction between the soul and the body, the physical and the spiritual. They tell us that there is no wholeness without sex, no authentic love without the feel and touch of the physical body. The blues affirm the authenticity of sex as the bodily expression of black soul.

The blues are not profane in any negative sense and neither are they immoral. They deal with the truth of human existence and the kinds of difficulties black people experience trying to hold themselves together. They tell us about their strengths and weaknesses, their joys and sorrows, their love and hate. And because they expressed their most intimate and precious feelings openly, they were able to survive as a community amid very difficult circumstances. They sang together, prayed together, and slept together. It was sometimes sweet and sometimes bitter; but they could make it because they tried; they "kept on pushing," looking for that new black humanity.

White people obviously cannot understand the love that black people have for each other. People who enslave humanity cannot understand the meaning of human freedom; freedom comes only to those who struggle for it in the context of the community of the enslaved. People who destroy physical bodies with guns, whips, and napalm cannot know the power of physical love. Only those who have been hurt can appreciate the warmth of love that proceeds when persons touch, feel, and embrace each other. The blues are openness to feeling and the emotions of physical love.

The Blues and Social Protest

Much has been said about the absence of social protest in the blues.[24] As Samuel Charters put it: "The blues do not try to express an attitude toward the separateness of Negro life in America. Protest is only a small thread in the blues."[25] There is some truth in Charters' observation. The blues do not *openly* condemn white society, and there is little *direct* complaint *to* white people about the injustice of segregation. But my difficulty with Charters' interpretation and others like it is the implied and often stated conclusion that the absence of open attack upon white society means that black people accepted their oppressed condition. As Paul Oliver openly states: "That the number of protest blues is small is in part the result of the Negro's acceptance of the stereotypes that have been cut for him."[26]

Assuming from the absence of open protest that black people internalized the values of white society and thus accepted the injustice committed against them reminds us of a similar view held regarding the spirituals. Since I have already made my objection to that kind of interpretation, there is no need to rehearse it here. It is enough to observe that white recorders and interpreters should know that blues men and women would have to be very naive to couch the blues in white categories of protest. Moreover, if they did, they would not likely sing them in recording studios! Deception was present not only during slavery but is still with us today, and it will continue to exist as long as there are white people in power who define law and order according to white supremacy and black inferiority. This simple fact seems to have been overlooked by even the most sensitive white interpreters of the blues.

In order to understand the black reaction to the social restrictions on the black community as reflected in the blues, it is necessary to view the blues from the perspective of black people's attempt to survive in a very hostile white society. The blues are not political treatises, and neither are they radical statements on social revolution. (It is safe to assume that blues people did not read Karl Marx.) The blues are statements *of* and *for* black people who are condemned to live in an extreme situation of oppression without any political leverage for defining their existence. The blues attempt to deal with the question: How can we black people survive in a world of white racism and hate? This question defines the sociological and theological background for an interpretation of the blues.

> Feeling tomorrow, like I feel today,
> If I feel tomorrow, like I feel today,
> I'll pack my suitcase, make my get away.

Consider the blues "Another Man Done Gone," which was created by Vera Hall, "a peaceloving cook and washerwoman and a pillar of the choir in her Baptist Church."[27] This blues is about chains, bloodhounds, prisons, and the need to escape the harsh realities of inhumanity. "It is enigmatic, full of silent spaces, speaking of the night and of a man slippin' by in the night." Then "you see his face, you know him, but at the same time you put him out of your mind, so that when the white man asks after him, you can say: 'I didn't know his name, I don't know where he's gone.' "[28] This song is a moving description of the blues feeling. It is not romantic about politics, nor is it evidence that black people accepted white rules and regulations as a definition of their being. This song is about the *togetherness* of the black community in view of the county farm and the chains.

> Another man done gone,
> Another man done gone,
> From the county farm
> Another man done gone.
>
> I didn't know his name,
> I didn't know his name,
> I didn't know his name,
> I didn't know his name.
>
> He had a long chain on,
> He had a long chain on,
> He had a long chain on,
> He had a long chain on.
>
> He killed another man,
> He killed another man,
> He killed another man,
> He killed another man.
>
> I don't know where he's gone,
> I don't know where he's gone,
> I don't know where he's gone,
> I don't know where he's gone.

Radical social protest assumes that the victimizers of human beings have a conscience and that the victims have the political leverage to publicize societal wrongs committed against them. But black people had little evidence that white people had a conscience and thus could hear their cries and moans. And they certainly did not possess the needed social and political power to verbalize the injustice of white people against the black community. What were black people to do when the slightest expression of social resentment could mean death? Without political freedom or the means of achieving it, many blacks turned to the blues for identity and survival. As Ralph Ellison has put it: "For the art—the blues, the spirituals, the jazz, the dance—was what we had in place of freedom."[29] The blues were techniques of survival and expressions of courage. They tell us about the contradictions that black people experienced and what they did to overcome them.

> They say we are the Lawd's children, I don't say that
> 　　ain't true,
> They say we are the Lawd's children, I don't say that
> 　　ain't true,
> But if we are the same like each other, ooh, well,
> 　　well, why do they treat me like they do?
>
> I want to live on children, children, I would like to
> 　　see,
> I want to live on children, children, I would like to
> 　　see,
> What will become of us, ooh, well, by nineteen and
> 　　fifty-three.
>
> Some of the Good Lawd's children, some of them
> 　　ain't no good,
> Some of the Good Lawd's children, some of them
> 　　ain't no good,
> Some of them are the devil, ooh, well, well, and won't
> 　　help you if they could.
>
> Some of the Good Lawd's children kneel upon their
> 　　knees and pray,

> Some of the Good Lawd's children kneel upon their
>   knees and pray,
> You serve the devil in the night, ooh, well, and serve
>   the Lawd in the day.

Black people were not oblivious to the fact of "Colored Only" and "White Only" signs on toilets, water fountains, and restaurants. They knew about friends and relatives who were beaten or lynched. They experienced the quiet nights of waiting for a brother or a father to come home and not knowing whether he had been permanently detained by a white mob looking for entertainment. They did not sing about it much, at least not directly. But the experience was present in the mood and style of the blues. The despair and loneliness were there, and the "tears came rolling down."

> I'm awful lonesome, all alone and blue,
> I'm awful lonesome, all alone and blue,
> Ain't got no body to tell my troubles to.

The political significance of the blues is not very impressive to those who have not experienced black servitude. Neither is it impressive to persons who are fascinated by modern theories of political revolution. But for black people who live the blues, who experience and share that history with their black fathers and mothers, the blues are examples of Black Power and the courage to affirm black being. Ellison is right:

> Any people who could endure all that brutalization and keep together, who could undergo such dismemberment and resuscitate itself, and endure until it could take the initiative in achieving its own freedom is obviously more than the sum of its brutalization. Seen in this perspective, theirs has been one of the great triumphs of the human spirit in modern times, in fact, in the history of the world.[30]

The Blues and Hope

Related to black suffering and the transcendent affirmation of being is the idea of the future, the not-yet of black existence.

The question is: How are the blues related to the hope and future of the black community? It is a commonly held opinion that there is no hope in the blues. Taking their clue from the "non-religious" perspective of the songs and the political disfranchisement of black people, some critics say that these songs represent black people's acceptance of their oppressed condition. According to this interpretation, the blues represent complete despair and utter hopelessness.

I think this interpretation needs to be re-evaluated in the light of the blues themselves and the cultural environment that created them. It is true that hopelessness is an authentic aspect of the blues' experience, and despair is a central theme in the blues. It was not possible for black people to experience the disappointment of post-Civil War America and not know the meaning of despair. Like the spirituals, the blues are not romantic; they do not camouflage the reality of social oppression. Oppression is real, and it often appears to the black community that there is little that can be done about it. It is this feeling of helplessness that produces the blues. The blues are that mood which owes its origins to powerlessness in the face of trouble.

> Sometimes I feel like nothin', somethin' th'owed
> away,
> Sometimes I feel like nothin', somethin' th'owed
> away,
> Then I get my guitar and play the blues all day.

> Money's all gone, I'm so far from home,
> Money's all gone, I'm so far from home,
> I just sit here and cry and moan.

The despair is real, not imagined. It is clear that the blues singer is searching for a reason to live, for purpose and meaning in existence. And the external realities of oppression seem to have gotten the best of him. And he lifts up his voice again:

> Ninety-nine years so jumpin' long,
> To be here rollin' and cain' go home.

> Don't yo go worrin' about forty [the years of the
>   prison sentence]
> Cause in five years you'll be dead.
>
> If you don't believe my buddy's dead,
> Just look at that hole in my buddy's head.
>
> Great gawdamighty, folks feelin' bad,
> Lost everything they ever had.

On the basis of these verses alone, it would be foolish to discount the presence of despair and hopelessness in the blues. But it is important to point out that despair is not the whole picture. For underneath the despair there is also a firm hope in the possibility of black people's survival despite their extreme situation of oppression. That is why blacks also sing: "Times is bad, but dey won't be bad always." Why? Because times "gotta get better 'cause dey cain't get w'us."

The hope of the blues is grounded in the historical reality of the black experience. The blues express a belief that one day things will not be like what they are today. This is why buses, railways, and trains are important images in the blues. Each symbolizes motion and the possibility of leaving the harsh realities of an oppressive environment. "Ef ah kin jes grab me a handfulla freight train—ah'll be set." The blues emphasize movement, the possibility of changing the present reality of suffering.

> I'd rather drink muddy water, sleep in a hollow log,
> Dan to stay in this town, treated like a dirty dog.
> Sitting here wondering would a matchbox hold my
>   clothes,
> I ain't got so many, and I got so far to go.
>
> I'm got a mind to ramble, a mind for to leave this
>   town.

The blues are a lived experience, an encounter with the contradictions of American society but a refusal to be conquered

by it. They are despair only in the sense that there is no attempt
to cover up reality. The blues recognize that black people have
been hurt and scared by the brutalities of white society. But
there is also hope in what Richard Wright calls the "endemic
capacity to live."[31] This hope provided the strength to survive,
and also an openness to the intensity of life's pains without being
destroyed by them. This is why Lonnie Johnson could sing:

> People is raisin' 'bout hard times, tell me what it's
> all about,
> People is hollerin' 'bout hard times, tell me what's it
> all about,
> Hard times don't worry me, I was broke when it first
> started out.
>
> Friends, it could be worser, you don't seem to under-
> stand,
> Friends, it could be worser, you don't seem to under-
> stand,
> Some is cryin' with a sack of gold under each arm
> and a loaf of bread in each hand.
>
> People ravin' 'bout hard times, I don't know why they
> should,
> People ravin' 'bout hard times, I don't know why they
> should;
> If some people was like me, they didn't have no
> money when times was good.

While the blues recognized poverty:

> Pocketbook was empty,
> My heart was full of pain.

Yet black people did not let such sociological realities define
the status of their being:

> When you lose your money,
> don't lose your mind.

In order to affirm being, a people must create forms for the expression of being and project it with images that reflect their perceptions of reality. They must take the structure of reality and subject it to the conditions of life—its pain, sorrow, and joy That black people could sing the blues, describing their sorrows and joys, meant that they were able to affirm an authentic hope in the essential worth of black humanity.

> My burden's so heavy, I can't hardly see,
> Seems like everybody is down on me,
> An' that's all right, I don't worry, oh, there will be a
>   better day.

The better day is not naive optimism. It is simply the will to be.

Unlike the spirituals, the hope of the blues is not located in the concept of heaven. "One cannot continually ride in chariots to God when the impact of slavery is so ever present and real."[32] The blues ground black hope firmly in history and do not plead for life after death. Even in death, there is no retreat from the willingness to accept the consequences of life. The bluesman only made one simple request:

> Well, there's one kind favor I ask of you,
> One kind favor I ask of you,
> Lord, there's one kind favor I ask of you,
> Please see that my grave is kept clean.

In sum, when the blues people are "standin' here looking one thousand miles away," they are looking for a home that is earthly *and* eschatological. Home would always be more than a plot of land, more than a lover, family and friends—though it would include these. Home would be the unrestricted affirmation of self and the will to protect self from those who would destroy self. It would be self-reliance and self-respect. In short, home could only be freedom, and the will to create a new world for the people I love.

Well, I'm going to buy me a little railroad of my own,
Well, I'm going to buy me a little railroad *all* my *own*,
Ain't going to let nobody ride but the chocolate-to-
the-bone.

A Concluding Reflection

Both the spirituals and the blues are the music of black people. They should not be pitted against each other, as if they are alien or radically different. One does not represent good and the other bad, one sacred and the other secular. Both partake of the *same* black experience in the United States.

Living under the harsh reality of slavery and segregation, the spirituals and the blues tell what black people did to keep together and endure. Blacks have always known that they were more than the little black sambos that whites imagined them to be. But it is one thing to know that you are a human being and quite another to create a world so that your humanity can be acknowledged. Through the power of human imagination, defined by their struggle against slavery and segregation, blacks created a separate world for themselves—a world defined by justice and peace, where women, men, and their children can freely love and be loved.

Music has been and continues to be the most significant creative art expression of African-Americans. Blacks sing and play music (in their churches and at juke-joint parties) as a way of coping with life's contradictions and of celebrating its triumphs. We sing when we are happy and when we are sad; when we get a job and when we lose one; when we protest for our rights and when the formal achievement of them makes no difference in the quality of our life. Singing is the medium through which we talk to each other and make known our perspectives on life to the world. It is our way of recording and reflecting on our experiences—the good and the bad, the personal and the political, the sacred and the secular.

Most blacks do not acknowledge these dualisms. They believe that reality is one. The spirituals and the blues record black people's feelings—their hopes and disappointments, their dreams and nightmares. We must view them as two artistic expressions of the same black experience.

In this book, I have told only a small part of a much larger musical story. Gospel music replaced the spirituals as the most dominant music in the churches and jazz followed the blues— all communicating strong messages about love and hate, right and wrong, God and the world. Today a new form of musical discourse has emerged in the black community. It's called "rap" music. It is a musical-talk, extremely popular among young people who are searching for meaning in a world that has no place for them.

Whatever form black music takes, it is always an expression of black life in America and what the people must do to survive with a measure of dignity in a society which seems bent on destroying their right to be human beings. The fact that black people keep making music means that we as a people refuse to be destroyed. We refuse to allow the people who oppress us to have the last word about our humanity. The last word belongs to us and music is our way of saying it. Contrary to popular opinion, therefore, the spirituals and the blues are not songs of despair or of a defeated people. On the contrary, they are songs which represent one of the great triumphs of the human spirit.

Notes

Introduction

1. LeRoi Jones, *Black Music* (New York: William Morrow & Co., 68), p. 183.
2. Cited in Phyl Garland, *The Sound of Soul* (Chicago: Henry Regnery Co., 1969), p. 104.
3. Cited in Ben Sidran, *Black Talk* (New York: Holt, Rinehart & Winston, 1971), p. 18.

1. Interpretations of the Black Spirituals

1. William Francis Allen, Charles P. Ware, and Lucy McKim Garrison, *Slave Songs of the United States* (New York: A. Simpson and Co., 1867), p. i. This book was the first systematic collection of the slave songs. Before this collection, Charlotte Forten had recorded a few songs on Saint Helena Island in 1864. Thomas Wentworth Higginson wrote an article in *The Atlantic Monthly* (1867), in which he included several spirituals that were sung by black soldiers in his regiment. Later (1871) he wrote his *Army Life in a Black Regiment* (Boston: Beacon Press, 1962) and included a chapter on the black spirituals. But it was not until 1871 that these songs became widely known, when a group of Fisk University students made a tour under the leadership of George White.
The Allen, Ware, and Garrison collection is an excellent source for the lyrics of the spirituals; as are also the books of James Johnson and John Work. The book of Odum and G. Johnson, and of Brown are useful. All these books will be referred to in this chapter.
2. Allen, pp. i-ii.
3. Cited in Henry E. Krehbiel, *Afro-American Folksongs* (New York: G. Schirmer, 1914), p. 1.
4. Krehbiel, p. 12.
5. Krehbiel, p. 22.

6. John W. Work, *The Folk Song of American Negro Spirituals* (Nashville: Fisk University Press, 1915), pp. 29-30.

7. James Weldon Johnson and J. Rosamond Johnson, *The Books of American Negro Spirituals* (New York: Viking Press, 1925), I, 13.

8. Johnson, I, 15.

9. See his "The Negro Spirituals" in his *The New Negro* (New York: Atheneum, 1969), pp. 199-200. Originally published in 1925. See also his *The New Negro and His Music* and *Negro Art: Past and Present* (New York: Arno Press, 1969). Originally published 1936.

10. Newman White, *American Negro Folk Songs* (Hatboro, Pennsylvania: Folklore Associates, Inc., 1928).

11. Guy Johnson, *Folk Culture on St. Helena Island* (Chapel Hill: The University of North Carolina Press, 1930); Howard Odum and Guy Johnson, *The Negro and His Songs* (Chapel Hill: The University of North Carolina Press, 1925).

12. George Pullen Jackson, *White Spirituals in the Southern Uplands* (Chapel Hill: The University of North Carolina Press, 1933).

13. Melville Herskovits, *The Myth of the Negro Past* (Boston: Beacon Press, 1958). Originally published in 1911. Despite the fact that this book is over thirty years old, it is still the most informed study on the subject. And it is difficult to defend the absence of Africanism in black religion after reading it.

14. Sterling Brown, "The Spirituals" in Langston Hughes and Arna Bontemps (eds.), *The Book of Negro Folklore* (New York: Dodd, Mead and Co., 1958), p. 283. See also his "Negro Expressions: Spirituals, Seculars, Ballads, and Work Songs" in August Meier and Elliot Rudwick, *The Making of Black America*, Vol. II (New York: Atheneum, 1969); "Folk Literature" in Sterling Brown, Arthur Davis, and Ulysses Lee, *The Negro Caravan* (New York: Arno Press, 1970). Originally published in 1941. See also *Negro Poetry and Drama* and *The Negro in American Fiction* (New York: Atheneum, 1969). Originally published in 1937.

15. W. E. B. DuBois, *The Souls of Black Folk* (New York: Fawcett Publications, 1961), p. 182.

16. DuBois, p. 183.

17. DuBois, p. 189.

18. DuBois, p. 17.

19. John Lovell, "The Social Implications of the Negro Spiritual" in Bernard Katz (ed.), *The Social Implications of Early Negro Music in the United States* (New York: Arno Press, 1969), p. 136. Originally published in 1939.

20. Lovell, p. 129.

21. Lovell, p. 132.

22. Lovell, p. 133.

23. Lovell, p. 134.

24. Lovell, pp. 134, 135.

25. Lovell, p. 136.

26. Lovell, p. 136.

27. Miles Mark Fisher, *Negro Slave Songs in the United States* (New York: Citadel Press, 1953), p. xi.

28. Fisher, p. 183.

29. Fisher, p. 1.

30. See Fisher, p. 27f.

31. See Fisher, p. 41.

32. See Fisher, pp. 66-67.

33. Howard Thurman, *The Negro Spiritual Speaks of Life and Death* (New York: Harper and Row, 1947), p. 12. See also his *Deep River* (Port Washington, New York: Kennikat Press, 1969). Originally published in 1945.

34. Thurman, pp. 14-15.

35. Thurman, p. 13.

36. Thurman, p. 12.

37. One possible exception is J. Garfield Owens, *All God's Chillun*, (Nashville: Abingdon Press, 1971). Although his interpretation has some theological insights, his book is basically sermon meditations and does not fall in the strict category of theology. His interpretation is not significantly different from Howard Thurman's; and there is no need to discuss it in this chapter.

Another interesting exception is the work of Theo Lehmann, an East German theologian. In an article "A Cry of Hope—The Negro Spirituals" (see Christian Duquoc (ed.), *Dimensions of Spirituality* [New York: Herder and Herder, 1970], pp. 125-133) Lehmann says that the spirituals are an affirmation of hope for freedom on earth and in heaven. However, like Mays, his emphasis is clearly on the otherworldly dimensions of the songs and he fails to capture the *ambiguity* of the black religious experience. While recognizing the close similarity between the psalms and the spirituals, he says: "Whereas Psalm 137 ... ends on a note of hatred and vengeance, the songs of the negro slaves ... rise up in pure praise of God and contain no trace of hatred of the oppressor and no indication of any desire for vengeance. These songs were born of the very spirit of Christ, who suffered without hating his oppressors" (p. 130). Of course, there is some truth in that observation, but it is nonetheless quite misleading. It not only makes theological assumptions about Christ that many slaves did not share but also fails to take with significant seriousness the role of spirituals in insurrection in which many whites were killed. While I do not say that hate was a central focus of the spirituals; yet unless the spirituals are directly related to historical strivings for earthly freedom, they will be misunderstood. Statements like, slaves accepted "the faith of their oppressors" (p. 126), must be carefully guarded. See also Lehmann's book *Negro Spirituals, Geschichte un Theologie* (Berlin, 1965).

38. Benjamin Mays, *The Negro's God* (New York: Atheneum, 1968), p. 21. Originally published in 1938.

39. Mays, pp. 21, 25.

40. Mays, p. 21.

41. Mays, pp. 23-24.

42. Mays, p. 28.

43. Mays, p. 26.

2. The Black Spirituals and Black Experience

1. B. A. Botkin (ed.), *Lay My Burden Down* (Chicago: The University of Chicago Press, 1945), p. 89.

2. Botkin, p. 90.

3. Botkin, p. 73.

4. Cited in Kenneth Stampp, *The Peculiar Institution* (New York: Vintage Books, 1956), p. 430.

5. The extent of self-hatred is difficult to measure. Scholars are divided on the issue. For example Stanley Elkins, *Slavery: A Problem in American Institutional and Intellectual Life* (Chicago: The University of Chicago Press, 1959) and Ulrich B. Phillips, *American Negro Slavery* (New York, 1918) contend that self-hatred was complete, and slaves shared happily the values of white masters. Herbert Aptheker, *American Negro Slave Revolts* (New York: International Publishers, 1943), Kenneth Stampp, *The Peculiar Institution*, and black historians such as Sterling Stuckey, "Through the Prism of Folklore," in J. Chametzky and S. Kaplan, *Black and White in American Culture* (Amherst: University of Massachusetts Press, 1969) and Vincent Harding, "Religion and Resistance Among Antebellum Negroes, 1800-1860" in *The Making of Black America*, Vol. I (Meier and Rudwick, eds.) do not think that self-hatred was complete. I think that the issue is not whether self-hate was present. As Stuckey says: "It should . . . be asserted . . . that blacks could not have survived the grim experience of slavery unscathed." The question is whether "in their struggle to control self-lacerating tendencies, the scales were tipped toward a despair so consuming that most slaves, in time, became reduced to the level of 'Sambos' " (p. 173).

Though black religion as reflected in the spiritual and other folk material is compensatory, it is not certain how many blacks accepted the *literal* interpretation of the songs. My research leads me to conclude that the literalists were in the minority and not the majority as is often supposed. That is, they devised a "literalism" which did not conflict with their humanity. Aside from the evidence of numerous slave revolts (See H. Aptheker, *American Negro Slave Revolts*), the exodus of enough slaves to necessitate the Fugitive Slave Law of 1850, the harsh slave codes throughout the south, and the laws banning the worship of blacks unless authorized whites were present, it must be remembered that not all slaves chose to risk their lives in an insurrection; and that did not mean that they accepted the values of their masters. The vast majority of slaves chose other forms of resistance — one of which was to sing songs with double meanings. Frederick Douglass and Harriet Tubman reported about the double meanings in spirituals. Then there are the folk tales and sayings which are packed full of deceptive meanings about the triumph of the weak over the strong. (See Arna Bontemps and Langston Hughes (eds.), *The Book of Negro Folklore* (New York: Dodd, Mead & Co., 1965) and Zora Neale Hurston, *Mules and Men* (Philadelphia: J. B. Lippincott, 1935).

To conclude that the majority of slaves accepted the values of masters because they did not commit suicide by attacking the U.S. government is like saying blacks today accept white values because they do not belong to the Black Panther Party. That simply is not true. If we are to interpret rightly the minds of black slaves, we must feel our way into their world, becoming sensitive to the many ways they resisted white slaveholders without losing their lives. More will be said about the mind of the slaves later.

6. Cited in Vincent Harding, "Religion and Resistance Among Antebellum Negroes 1800–1860" in *The Making of Black America*, Vol. I, edited by August Meier and Elliot Rudwick (New York: Atheneum, 69), p. 181.

7. Cited in Stampp, p. 156.

8. Donald Matthews, *Slavery and Methodism?* (Princeton: Princeton University Press, 1965), p. 87.

9. Of course, there may be notable exceptions. The Quakers' stand against slavery is widely known. And during the late eighteenth century Methodists, Baptists, and Presbyterians spoke out against slavery. But after the solid entrenchment of slavery in the south with the invention of the cotton gin, most denominations did not follow through on their earlier pronouncements. The report of the Committee on Slavery to the Methodist General Conference in 1816 was typical: "The commit-

tee to whom was referred the business of slavery beg leave to report, that they have taken the subject into serious consideration, and, after mature deliberation, they are of the opinion that under the present existing circumstances in relation to slavery, little can be done to abolish a practice so contrary to the principles of moral justice. They are sorry to say that the evil appears to be past remedy; and they are led to deplore the destructive consequences which have already accrued, and are likely to result therefrom." (Cited in Robert T. Handy, "Negro Christianity" in Jerald C. Brauer, *Reinterpretation in American Church History* (Chicago: The University of Chicago Press, 1968), p. 94).

While most denominations did not support the abolitionist movement during the nineteenth century, there were some ministers involved in it. Theodore Dwight Weld was an example. See his *The Bible Against Slavery: An Inquiry into the Patriarchal and Mosaic Systems on the Subject of Human Rights*; a selection is in Osofsky, *The Burden of Race*, p. 87f.

10. See Arna Bontemps, *Black Thunder* (Boston: Beacon Press, 1968); John O. Killens, *The Trial Record of Denmark Vesey* (Boston: Beacon Press, 1970); Herbert Aptheker, *Nat Turner's Slave Rebellion* (New York: Grove Press, 1966); John H. Clarke, *William Styron's Nat Turner* (Boston: Beacon Press, 1968).

11. See Earl Conrad, *Harriet Tubman* (New York: P. S. Ericksson, 1969).

12. Henry H. Garnet, *An Address to the Slaves of the United States of America* (New York: Arno Press, 1969).

13. There are many slave narratives which were written during the nineteenth century. They were important documents used by the abolitionists in the fight against slavery. It is true that most of them bear the stylistic changes of the white abolitionists and some were fictional. But many are authentic and they include the narratives of Henry Bibb, William Wells Brown, and Solomon Northup in Gilbert Osofsky (ed.), *Puttin' on Ole Massa* (New York: Harper Torchbooks, 1969); the Narratives of Lunsford Lane, Moses Grandy, J. W. C. Pennington, and Jacob Stroyer are in William Loren Katz (ed.), *Five Slave Narratives* (New York: Arno Press 1969); Gustavus Vassa and William and Ellen Craft experiences are in Arno Bontemps (ed.). *Great Slave Narratives* (Boston: Beacon Press, 1969); the most widely read account is Frederick Douglass' account of his life in the *Life and Times of Frederick Douglass* (New York: Collier Books, 1962). An excellent account of ex-slaves' perception of their experiences (in their own words) is found in B. A. Botkin (ed.), *Lay My Burden Down* (Chicago: The University of Chicago Press, 1945).

14. Cited in Stampp, p. 112.

15. Cited in Charles H. Nichols, *Many Thousand Gone* (Bloomington: Indiana University Press, 1963), p. 47.

16. Stampp, pp. 108-109.

17. Stampp, p. 128.

18. Cited in Julius Lester, *To Be a Slave* (New York: Dell, 1970), pp. 100-101.

19. See Charles Ball's comment cited by Lester, p. 100-101.

20. Cited in Lester, p. 100.

21. "Narrative of Lunsford Lane" in Katz (ed.), *Five Slave Narratives*, p. 31.

22. Cited in Stampp, pp. 86-87.

23. Cited in Stampp, p. 87.

24. Stampp, pp. 334-335.

25. See Vincent Harding, "Religion and Resistance Among Antebellum Negroes," in August Meier and Elliott Rudwick (eds.), *The Making of Black America* (New York: Atheneum, 1969), p. 189.

26. For an analysis of the relationship of the spirituals and Africanisms, see Melville Herskovits, *The Myth of the Negro Past*, Chapter VII; Stampp, p. 362f.

27. Cited in Lucy McKim Garrison, "Songs of the Port Royal 'Contrabands,'" in Bernard Katz, *The Social Implications of Early Negro Music in the United States*, p. 10.

28. Comment by Guy Johnson of the University of North Carolina, cited in Sterling Stuckey, "Through the Prism of Folklore," in *Black and White in American Culture*, p. 172.

3. God and Jesus Christ in the Black Spirituals

1. I have already referred to the otherworldly emphasis in these songs. But the stress on the next world does not detract from my main point. The eschatological emphasis merely postpones divine liberation and does not deny it. Chapter 5 will deal with this aspect. My present concern is only to stress the emphasis on divine liberation, whether historical or eschatological.

2. Karl Marx and Friedrich Engels, *On Religion* (New York: Schocken Books, 1964), p. 42.

3. Fisher, *Negro Slave Songs*, pp. 27-28, 66-67, 181-185.

4. Fisher, p. 108. It is important to note that Fisher is quoting the conservative estimate of a southern historian.

5. See Fisher, Chapter 4. He notes that the spirituals were used to convene secret meetings among slaves, and the colony of Virginia prohibited them as early as 1676 (p. 29, 66ff.). Most colonies joined Vir-

ginia in outlawing the secret meetings, but "neither outlawry nor soldiery prevented them from having hemispheric significance" (p. 67).

6. A strong advocate of this position is Newman White, *American Negro Folk Songs*. For the opposite position, see Sterling Brown "The Spirituals" in Hughes and Bontemps, *Book of Negro Folklore*, p. 286f.

7. James Weldon Johnson, *God's Trombones* (New York: The Viking Press, 1927), pp. 4-5.

8. B. A. Botkin (ed.), *Lay My Burden Down* (Chicago: The University of Chicago Press, 1945), p. 26.

9. James Miller McKim "Negro Songs" in Bernard Katz, *The Social Implications of Early Negro Music in the United States*, p. 2.

10. Thomas Wentworth Higginson, *Army Life in a Black Regiment*, p. 219.

11. Sterling Brown, "Negro Folk Expression: Spirituals, Seculars, Ballads and Work Songs" in Meier and Rudwick, *The Making of Black America*, p. 213.

12. Botkin, *Lay My Burden Down*, p. 125.

13. James Weldon Johnson, *The Second Book of American Negro Spirituals*, p. 14.

14. Johnson, p. 15.

15. Howard Thurman, *Deep River*, p. 16.

16. In the history of theology, the contemporary presence of the Son and the Father was spoken of in terms of the Holy Spirit. But in the spirituals, there was hardly any mention of the work of the Spirit. Perhaps this was due to the tendency of thinking of the Spirit as an "it" or "nonperson." The slaves personalized their religion and tended to think of God as someone they could walk and talk with, telling him about their difficulties.

4. God and Black Suffering

1. See Joseph Washington, *Black Religion* (Boston: Beacon Press, 1964); E. Franklin Frazier, *The Negro Church in America* (New York: Shocken Books, 1964).

2. Sterling Brown, "Negro Folk Expression: Spirituals, Seculars, Ballads and Work Songs" in A. Meier and E. Rudwick, *The Making of Black America*, Vol. II, pp. 215, 216.

3. "Bishop Daniel Alexander Payne's Protestation of American Slavery," *Journal of Negro History*, Vol. LII (1967), p. 63. Emphasis in original.

4. Payne, pp. 63-64.

5. Nathaniel Paul, "An Address Delivered on the Celebration of

the Abolition of Slavery in the State of New York, July 5, 1827" in Carter G. Woodson, *Negro Orators and Their Orations* (New York: Russell and Russell, 1969), p. 69.

6. Paul, p. 69.

7. Howard Thurman, *Negro Spiritual Speaks of Life and Death*, pp. 19-20. See also Herskovits, *Myth of the Negro Past*, p. 200f.

8. See John and Alan Lomax, *Folk Songs U.S.A.*, p. 424f.

9. Howard Odum and Guy B. Johnson, *The Negro and His Songs*, p. 39.

10. Lovell, "The Social Implications of the Negro Spiritual," p. 134f.

11. Thurman, *Negro Spiritual Speaks of Life and Death*, pp. 31-32.

5. The Meaning of Heaven in the Black Spirituals

1. See Fisher, *Negro Slave Songs*, Chapters 1-4.

2. Frederick Douglass, *Life and Times of Frederick Douglass* (New York: Collier Books, 1962), p. 159. A reprint of the 1892 revised edition.

3. Sarah Bradford, *Harriet Tubman: The Moses of Her People* (New York: Corinth Books, 1961), pp. 27-28. A reprint of the second edition of 886.

4. Bradford, p. 30.

5. Bradford, pp. 31-32.

6. Bradford, p. 33.

7. Earl Conrad, *Harriet Tubman*, p. 77.

8. Cited in Conrad, p. 78, from Richard Randall, "Fighting Sons of the Unemployed," *The Sunday Worker Progressive Weekly*, September 3, 1939, p. 2.

9. Howard Thurman, *Deep River*, p. 56.

10. Johannes B. Metz, "God Before Us Instead of a Theological Argument" in *Cross Currents*, Vol. XVIII, No. 3, Summer 1968.

11. Metz.

12. Gajo Petrovic, *Marx in the Mid-Twentieth Century* (New York: Doubleday and Co., 1967), p. 120. Italics in original.

13. Walter Benjamin as quoted in Herbert Marcuse, *One-Dimensional Man* (Boston: Beacon Press, 1964), p. 257.

14. Botkin, *Lay My Burden Down*, pp. 268-269.

15. N. H. Snaith, "Judge" in Alan Richardson (ed.), *A Theological Word Book of the Bible* (New York: Macmillan Co., 1950), p. 118.

16. Snaith.

6. The Blues: A Secular Spiritual

1. See LeRoi Jones, *Blues People* (New York: William Morrow and Company, 1963); Alain Locke, *The Negro and His Music* and *Negro Art:*

Past and Present (New York: Arno Press, 1069); Charles Keil, *Urban Blues* (Chicago: The University of Chicago Press, 1916); Phyl Garland, *The Sound of Soul* (Chicago: Henry Regnery Co., 1969); Harold Courlander, *Negro Folk Music U.S.A.* (New York: Columbia University Press 1961); Eileen Southern, *The Music of Black Americans* (New York: W. W. Norton, 1971); Rudi Blesh, *Shining Trumpets* (New York: Alfred Knopf, 1946); Paul Oliver, *The Meaning of the Blues* (New York: Collier Books, 1963) and *The Story of the Blues* (Philadelphia: Chilton Book Co. 1969); Samuel Charters, *The Bluesmen* (New York: Oak Publications 1967) and *The Poetry of the Blues* (New York: Avon, 1963); Russell Ames, *The Story of American Folk Song* (New York: Grosset and Dunlap 1960); and John A. and Alan Lomax, *Folk Song U.S.A.* The list of commentators on the blues could be extended but these are some of the important studies. For the lyrics, Oliver's *The Meaning of the Blues*, Charters' *Poetry of the Blues* and Sterling Brown's "The Blues" in *The Negro Caravan* and his "Blues" in L. Hughes and A. Bontemps, *Book of Negro Folklore* are the most useful.

2. Rudi Blesh, *Shining Trumpets*, p. 47.

3. Blesh, p. 48.

4. Brown, "Negro Folk Expression" in A. Meier and E. Rudwick, *The Making of Black America*, p. 215.

5. Brown in *Negro Caravan*, p. 426.

6. John W. Work, *American Negro Songs and Spirituals* (New York: Bonanza Books, 1940), p. 28.

7. Jones, *Blues People*, p. 62.

8. Cited in Russell Ames, *American Folk Song*, p. 262.

9. I am indebted to C. Eric Lincoln of Union Theological Seminary for this phrase.

10. Jones, *Blues People*, p. 142.

11. Jones, p. 80.

12. Cited in Samuel Charters, *Poetry of the Blues*, p. 58.

13. Cited in Charters, p. 17.

14. Cited in Charters.

15. Cited in Charters, p. 18.

16. Cited in Arnold Shaw, *The World of Soul* (New York: Coronet Communications, 1971), p. 31.

17. Cited in R. Ames, *American Folk Song*, p. 252.

18. Cited in A. Shaw, *World of Soul*, p. 38.

19. Cited in Paul Oliver, *The Blues Tradition* (New York: Oak Publications, 1970), p. 47.

20. Cited in E. Simms Campbell, "Blues" in Frederic Ramsey, Jr. (ed.) *Jazzmen* (New York: Harcourt Brace, and Co., 1939), pp. 110-111.

21. Cited in Charters, *Poetry of the Blues*, p. 18.

22. Cited in Tony Russell, *Blacks, Whites and Blues* (New York: Stein and Day, 1970), p. 77.

23. See Jones, *Blues People*, pp. 152, 153

24. See P. Oliver, *Meaning of the Blues*; S. Charters, *Poetry of the Blues*.

25. Charters, p. 12.

26. Oliver, p. 322.

27. John and Alan Lomax, *Folk Song U.S.A.*, p. 376.

28. Lomax, p. 377.

29. Ralph Ellison, *Shadow and Act* (New York: Signet Books, 1964), p. 247

30. Ellison, "A Very Stern Discipline," *Harpers* (March 1967), p. 84.

31. Richard Wright, "Forward," in Paul Oliver, *The Meaning of the Blues*, p. 9.

32. E. Simms Campbell, "Blues," in *Jazzmen*, p. 104.